MIND READER

MIND READER

UNLOCKING THE POWER
OF YOUR MIND
TO GET WHAT YOU WANT

LIOR SUCHARD

wm

WILLIAM MORROW
An Imprint of HarperCollins*Publishers*

All photographs courtesy of the author, with the exception of the following: insert pp. 1–4 courtesy of Melanie Fenton-Azulay.

HarperCollins books may be purchased for educational, business, or sales promotional use. For information please e-mail the Special Markets Department at SPsales@harpercollins.com.

FIRST EDITION

Designed by Aline C. Pace
Illustrations designed by Adam Johnson

Library of Congress Cataloging-in-Publication Data has been applied for.

ISBN 978-0-06-208737-9

19   OV/LSC   10 9

For Tal,

who fills me with happy thoughts.
I couldn't have done any of this without you.

CONTENTS

PREFACE

Mind Reader: Revealed

One night I was in Los Angeles with a friend and his family when a car followed us home from a party, slipping into the private gated community behind us. We darted into the house, wondering what to do, while the car parked across the street. There were four of us, and we decided to go back outside and investigate. Safety in numbers, we thought. But the moment we stepped into the darkness outside the house, a large man leapt out of the car and screamed, "Don't move. Whoever you are. Police." He was holding a gun. We've all seen it in movies but it's really, really scary when it's happening to you. Thoughts flew into my mind, none of them good. Then, almost before we knew it, there were six police cars, sirens blaring, and a helicopter circling overhead lighting up the sky. What was going on? The first policeman yelled at me, waving me forward. All around me lights were flashing and there was constant noise and movement but all I was looking at were guns. Within seconds I was handcuffed, my hands bound together in front then jerked up over my head. The policeman patted me down, not rough but purposeful. Invasive. I searched his face, his eyes, but didn't see anything. My mind was just filled with the word "why?" and choked up with fear. From my jacket pocket, he pulled out one broken spoon, a handful of long silver nails, one pencil, and one small notepad. He brandished the broken spoon right in my face like it was a weapon, yelling furiously, "What the hell? What the hell is this?" For a moment, I was silent. Shocked. "I'm, I'm a mind reader," I stuttered. "A mentalist. A performer?" He stared at me in disbelief, glared at the items in his hand, and then shook his head, telling me to balance on one leg.

It turned out that he thought I was driving drunk—I wasn't—and he called for backup when he saw four men start out of the house toward him. The point of the story is that all the officer found on me was a broken spoon, some long silver nails, a pencil, and a small notepad. The spoon had been broken in two with the power of my mind at a private party two hours before. The nails I would bend in practice to prepare for a Japanese TV show the next week. And the pencil and paper were for everyday mind stunts—you never know when you might need them. These items mean the world to me. Literally. They are the tools of my trade, and they have taken me from a small town in Israel to TV shows, live shows, private parties, lectures, business conventions, and trade shows in more than forty countries around the world.

When you're standing there, scared for your life, with

strange thoughts flashing through your mind, you find yourself reduced to your essence. While I balanced on one leg and
proved I wasn't drunk or dangerous, the policeman looked at
that broken spoon again and said, "A mind reader?"—his voice
suspicious, but his eyes open, vulnerable. I reached for my notebook and pencil, looked into his face, and scribbled something
down for myself. Then I asked him, "If I were to ask you to
think of a number between one and a hundred, what would it
be?" My fear was gone. He thought for a moment. "Twenty-
eight." I tore the paper from my notebook and gave it to him.
It said, "The policeman will say 28." He was blown away, grinning from ear to ear like a child.

My name is Lior Suchard, and I am a mentalist. I entertain
people by showing them the amazing power of the mind. I love
to see their eyes widen with surprise when I tell them what

they're thinking, or, even better, when I make them think what they're thinking. I love the positive energy that comes out of all my shows, my encounters, big and small, on the streets of Tel Aviv, at a TV show in Japan, or before eight hundred people in Vegas. No matter who someone is, they become like a child again when they experience that sense of wonder. It's why I do what I do, and my run-in with the policeman reminded me of that. If my essence is getting people to laugh and wonder with the help of a broken spoon, a handful of long silver nails, a notebook, and a pencil, then I'm okay with that. Besides, the experience gave me another cool story to tell, which is part of my essence, too. L.A. cops, huh?

MIND READER

ONE

Mentalism Revealed—Now I'll Have to Kill You

So what does a mentalist do? Right now, I'm incredibly busy performing all over the world: Las Vegas, New York, Los Angeles, Japan, South Africa, Russia, Europe, Israel, the list goes on. I've traveled to three different continents in one week. I sleep a lot on airplanes and carry several different phones. I never know who might call or when. It could be the king of Romania one week, Donna Karan or a high-tech maven the next; with Russian oligarchs in between just telling me to show up at a private airfield at a certain time. And, by the way, don't be late. I appear in many countries on TV talk shows, including Jay Leno, and sometimes they even invite me back. Including Jay Leno. I'm big in Japan. Go figure. I work at international corporate events and trade shows, for companies like Coca-Cola, Microsoft, BMW, and Omega. I'm invited into big-business conference rooms to break the ice before meetings, to make billionaires play nice—

and I'm invited to private Hollywood parties to entertain movie stars and their A-list friends. I've opened for Joan Rivers in Las Vegas, where I also have my own show. And yes, I'm welcome in Vegas as long as I stay out of the casinos. By the way, the stories about the black list are true!

Sometimes, when I happen to be at the beach or the market or the local diner, I perform. I just can't help myself. I'm walking down the street and before I know it I'm meeting someone and performing. I'm amazing them with my mind games and they're looking at me, wondering, "Oh my god, how did you do that?" It's fun. I love the energy. It's a whirlwind of an adventure, and everywhere I go I put in my best performance. I may have just arrived off a twelve-hour flight from hell, had a fight with my manager, my mother, and my girlfriend, but no one in the audience will sense it. I check my fatigue, my emotions at the door, and when I step onto the stage or enter a room, I turn my mind on full blast and become Lior Suchard Extreme, supernatural entertainer. Positive energy and human connection are everything to me. I live to show others how amazing the mind is and to make people laugh, to step outside of themselves and say, "Wow." Whether they're a Hollywood movie star, a CEO of a Fortune 500 company, or the person sitting across from me at the airport, it's all the same to me. I want people to wonder.

YOU'LL SEE THIS LOOK OF WONDER THAT I LOVE SO MUCH WHEN I HEAD TO THE BEACH AND TELL RANDOM PEOPLE THEIR BIRTH DATES. GO TO WWW.MINDREADERBOOK.COM/BIRTHDAY

So that's what this mentalist—or supernatural entertainer, as I sometimes call myself now—does when not evading the police. But maybe that doesn't really answer the question. What exactly does a mentalist do?

Well, in general and according to Wikipedia, the tradition of mentalists as stage performers goes back to the sixteenth century, but there are references to seers and oracles among the writings of the ancient Greeks. Mentalists demonstrate highly developed mental or intuitive abilities. That's certainly true for me. I wield my mind like a precision tool to read minds, influence thoughts, make predictions, and make objects move or bend without touching them (like the spoon and nails in my pocket). I could guess the name of your first love, first teacher, the name of your unborn child, your birth sign, the number you're thinking about. I can transfer feelings using the power of positive energy from one person to another. And I can guess your next question: "But please, Lior, how do you do that?"

During one of my performances, for a large company, a man called out exactly that question in the middle of the show: "But please, Lior, how do you do that?" When someone unexpectedly interrupts my show—and it happens more than you'd think—I try to keep the mood light. I don't want to punish them. So I looked at him, laughed, and said with a grin, "Sir, if I tell you, I'll have to kill you." There was gentle laughter in the audience, then silence as the audience's attention turned back to me, ready for my next act. But the man piped up again. "Then could you please tell my wife?" Everybody started to laugh like crazy. The guy had just asked me to kill his wife. Now I tell this story at every show.

But, in answer to the question—and without killing anybody—I'll say, basically, I use my five senses to create a "sixth sense." A sense of the mind. A sensitive intuition. Then I use this sense, in conjunction with a whole bunch of skills I've learned, to do the mind reading, persuasion, telekinesis, and other cool stuff. Skills like the power of suggestion, knowing how to read body language, persuasion, guided imagery, psychological analysis, and nonverbal communication. I put these techniques together in different combinations and I use them to direct and influence people and read minds. I take in crazy amounts of information and I implant information. I use my intuition a lot. That's what mentalism is about—it's a skill; in my case, probably partly genetic, partly learned. Everything I do is about using my mind in the best way I can, at the highest level that's possible.

Sometimes it can be hard to analyze and explain what I do, because I just do it. Like Nike. Think about love for a moment. When people are in love, they know what it feels like—it just happens and exists and makes perfect sense to them. They don't analyze it rationally. But a scientist could come along and explain that love is chemistry, that when we fall in love we experience a racing heart, flushed skin, and sweaty palms, because of the chemicals dopamine and norepinephrine that our bodies release. It doesn't sound so romantic anymore. And it doesn't explain all those other things about being in love: finishing each other's sentences, knowing what the other is going to say, that feeling of walking on air. It narrows something down to an exact science that maybe isn't an exact science.

Over the years, I've created metaphors for what I do as a

mentalist. I think the clearest way to explain is to concentrate on the way I use and focus my mind, as that is at the heart of everything I do. If you imagine the difference between a flashlight and a laser beam, you'll understand. Both are sources of light, but the laser beam is much more focused, so you can see more with it. Do more. If you flash a flashlight in your eyes, you'll be blinded for a moment, but a laser beam can cut diamond.

I believe it's the same with thought. When I'm working, my thoughts are really focused and powerful, and that's how I make things happen. I'm harnessing the power of my mind in a very conscious way. We actually sense thinking outside of the mind as we project our thoughts, all around us, not just inside our brains. I believe that everybody has transmitters to receive or send thoughts, but it's a question of how many people use them. We all use our minds differently. Think about it. Anyone can learn to play the piano, but not everyone will become Beethoven. What I do today as a mentalist is a combination of a gift and development of that gift.

However, being a mentalist is about more than mental skills—if you want to make it big in the entertainment business, anyway. There's another equally important component that goes along with the mental abilities. My father calls it a gene—the showman gene, or the performance gene. I'm lucky enough to have that, too. Over the years I've come to realize how important it is to what I do, and so I've taken special care to understand it and develop it. After all, there wouldn't be much entertainment value to my show if I just went up on stage, quietly read a few minds, mumbled shyly and awkwardly, shuffled around with my back turned to the audience, thanked you for coming, then ducked behind the curtain. You'd want your money back, and there certainly wouldn't be any positive feelings fluttering around at the end of the show. The success of my performances is probably based fifty percent on my mental skills—everybody likes to be wowed—but the other fifty percent is definitely for the show I put on: the close connection I create with the audience. The comic concepts, jokes and humor; the rapport I develop; that sense of positive energy. Everything goes hand in hand in my show and everyone is guaranteed a good time.

But why am I telling you this when you can step inside the theater and see me perform? Let me invite you to a show and you'll see for yourself the power of the mind. But, remember, if you ask me how I do it . . . I'll have to kill you.

Las Vegas, 2011

900 People

It's a few minutes before showtime. The audience settles, people are taking their seats and chatting quietly when suddenly the lights go out and complete darkness fills the auditorium. Anticipation builds. Silence. Then a blast of music and light. Velvet curtains sweep back across twenty-foot screens as a video begins to play. A deep voice reverberates, "Do you believe that someone can read your mind?" Images of me performing around the world flash across the screen: audiences in London, Hong Kong, Sydney, Moscow, and Paris laugh and gasp and their amazed reactions and looks of wonder fill the screen. The video introduces the in-your-face excitement and raw emotion to come, and the audience here in Vegas is captivated as they anticipate what's ahead for them in the next hour of my show. As the video screens fade to black, the voice continues, laying out the words dramatically, "Ladies and gentlemen, welcome Lior Suchard."

Drums roll and music blasts as I run out onto the stage, smiling, excited, my arms extended toward the audience. Behind me, colored lights splash across the huge screens while a spotlight follows me from one side of the stage to the other. Applause rolls toward me in waves, and I let it reverberate around the auditorium, washing over me, rebounding off the screens and back toward the audience. It's loud tonight, welcoming. Some people are standing, clapping, others getting to their feet now. There's a good crowd. A sold-out show. Already I can feel the energy in the air.

TO SEE A SHORT TRAILER OF MY WORLD TRAVELS AND THE REACTIONS OF DIFFERENT CULTURES GO TO: WWW.MINDREADERBOOK.COM/OPENING

"Hello, hello," I say over the noise. The applause continues but people start to settle, sitting down in their seats. "Good evening, everybody. Shhh." The applause fades away now. Faces are turned up expectantly toward me. I wait a moment, one beat, two. They're listening. Here we go. "So, do you believe someone can read your mind?" I address the whole audience, microphone in hand. They wait for my answer. "I guess we'll have to figure it out tonight." Gentle laughter. "Before I start I have to ask a question," I say, scanning the audience. I'm taking notes in my head, seeing who's here in a group, who's celebrating something, whether there are more men than women, the little details. "You! Over there. Say your name out loud."

The man answers, "John." He's about forty, casual, laid-back. "You are correct," I say. He laughs good-naturedly, and the rest of the audience follows suit. They're relaxing, settling back in their chairs for the show.

"Let me write something down for you," I say, hopping down into the audience and jogging over to John, who's sitting about six rows back. I look at his face while I'm writing on a whiteboard, holding it close to my chest so no one else can see. John looks interested, his gray eyes intelligent. Open-minded. I keep the board to myself for now. "So, if I were to ask you to say out loud a two-digit number, what would it be?"

All eyes in the audience turn to John now. He doesn't pause. He doesn't think long and hard. Right away, he says, "Twenty-four."

"That's amazing. I wrote down here, 'John will say 24,' " I say as I turn the whiteboard around and show John, then hold it up so everyone in the audience can see. I hear someone scream "Oh my god" in a distant row. Beside me, John is laughing with surprise, and the audience is impressed. "Thank you, John. Oh, and don't forget to get your check after the show. Next time say sixty-two, okay?"

John does a double take, before laughing loudly. "Just kidding," I say.

I head back to the middle of the stage, hold out my arms in welcome. The lights dance behind me, and there's a low rattle of drums. "So, good evening, ladies and gentlemen. My name is Lior Suchard and I deal with something very, very rare. I am a mind reader. This means that in the next few minutes you are going to experience a supernatural, entertaining adventure that will explore the great abilities of the human mind: mind-reading, influencing, nonverbal communication, ESP, and much, much more. You will not see sleight of hand here. In fact, if you see sleight of hand—then it means that it was not sleight of hand." Everyone laughs. I smile and laugh lightly along with the audience. They are warmed up and ready to have fun. "By the way, I'm terribly sorry about my bad English . . . but my accent is wonderful." Gentle laughter ripples across the audience. Some people are leaning forward toward the stage, expectant. Others relax in their chairs. I scan their faces, sensing their energy. They are all engaged.

"So, everyone, take a deep breath. It's time for me to try and read your thoughts." The music starts up, energetic and upbeat. I stride down from the stage and move among the audience, smiling, looking from left to right. "It's funny," I say. "Every time I do this, everybody goes, 'Noooo, please don't let him choose me.'" I'm still looking around, deciding whom to pick. A gray-haired man looks confident, while the woman in the next seat hides behind him. At the end of another row, I pause. People are laughing, smiling. One woman seems nervous but she smiles anyway. The woman next to her has lots of dark hair and looks eager. "Hmmm," I say. "What's your name?"

Bubbling with laughter, she says, "Shirley."

"Shirley, please join me on the stage! Give a big hand to Shirley." All the women in her row clap like crazy, especially the one who looked nervous. Maybe they're having a girls' night out?

I follow Shirley back onto the stage, soaking up all the applause as I go. We stand side by side. She pulls at her shirtsleeves and plays with a silver chain around her neck. "Hello, are you afraid of me?" She shakes her head so her hair dances. "You will be soon." Laughter. "By any chance, do you have a piece of paper and marker on you??"

Shirley laughs. "No."

"Okay, so I'll use mine." I'm addressing Shirley but also speaking to the audience, keeping them involved. "This is the first mind experiment. In a second I'll ask you to go outside . . . and don't come back. No, I'm just joking. " Shirley giggles. "So, you're going to go outside and write a name on the piece of paper. The name of someone you know who's not here, and that there's no chance in the world that I would know. Then fold up the paper and hide it deep in your pocket. Okay?"

Shirley nods enthusiastically and starts to walk away along the stage. The music plays to the beat of her footsteps while the spotlight shines down on her. Very dramatic. Very theatrical. "Now, it's very, very important that you do not let anyone follow you, that you don't let anyone peek and see what you wrote." All the time I'm saying this I'm walking right behind her, like a cartoon character, very close, peering over her shoulder. She senses me, turns, and laughs, then puts her hands on her hips as if she's telling me off. The audience likes that. She holds the piece of paper tightly in front of her, then heads off stage while I go back to the middle and look down into the audience. Then, as an afterthought, I call out to Shirley, "Please write on the left side underneath the special camera I installed there." There's a lot of warm, good-hearted laughter in response.

While we're waiting for Shirley to write the name, I turn back to the audience and address them, section by section. "Okay, my friends. This show is all about positive energy and that means that when Shirley comes back I want to hear you all applauding like crazy. All the guys shouting and cheering. All the women, bras in the air. Just kidding." Everyone cracks up, laughing loudly. "Shirley, take your time," I shout over the laughter and applause. "You have ten seconds."

That brings her back quickly and she half-walks, half-runs across the stage. She's a little flushed, excited by all the noise. "Ladies and gentlemen—please welcome: Shirley!" The music strikes up again, loud and cheerful, matching the atmosphere beautifully.

"Okay, so did anyone see anything written down?" I'm asking the audience. They're shaking their heads. "Good. Now, Shirley, look into my eyes." I gaze into her eyes for a few moments, getting quite close. She stands still. "Hmmmm," I start, "I can already sense something from you. It's a man or woman, right?" She and the audience laugh loudly.

"Okay, so please say out loud the word 'man.'"

"Man." She whispers it.

"Now say the word 'woman.'"

"Woman," she says, barely any louder.

I look directly into her eyes. "It's a man, right?"

Shirley nods and says, "Yes."

She looks very pleased. "But wait," I start. "It's not that impressive." I look out into the audience. "That guy over there is thinking to himself, 'Fifty-fifty,' right?" Everyone laughs. I turn back to Shirley. "Now think of the number of letters in the name. Don't say, just think. If you say it and then I reveal it, it's much less impressive for the audience." My voice is calm and I keep up the banter, but I'm focused now, energized. "So there are one . . . two . . . three . . . . four . . . it's four letters, right?"

"Yes!"

The audience starts in with applause but I hold up my hand and turn back to them. "No, no, no, don't applaud. He's still thinking: 'Lior, many men have four letters in their name.'" I move down off the stage and into the audience. "For example, what's your name?"

"Mike."

"You see, four letters. What's your name?"

"Jonathan." I stop short, counting on my fingers. "Never mind!"

Everyone's laughing now. Especially Shirley up on the stage. I bound up the steps to join her there, caught up in the energy of the audience. "So, Shirley, now comes the hard part. Imagine that he is here now, and you have to introduce him to me. You would say, 'Lior.' Please repeat after me. 'Lior, I would like you to meet.' " Shirley repeats the sentence then looks expectantly at me. "Then you would say his name, right?" She nods. "You would say, 'Andy,' " I say. Shirley's mouth opens wide in amazement and she clutches at her face.

"Yes!" she shouts. "Oh my god! Holy ****!"

"Really?" I say.

"Yes!" She's jumping around on the stage, her hands over her mouth. "That's amazing!" The audience is clapping like crazy.

Over their noise and energy, I shout, "Please give her a big round of applause." The music starts to play while Shirley, still holding her mouth, heads back to her seat. Her friends leap to their feet to welcome her back, still applauding.

I'm back in the middle of the stage and I walk out to the very edge to address the audience. "Now I want to stop the show completely. I need you to listen carefully, very carefully, and you have to capture this moment in your mind. Don't forget what you see!" I pause to let the message sink in. "I need someone who has some money." Some people in the audience are laughing, but others have their hands in the air. I choose one of these, an eager-looking guy in a nice suit.

"You, sir, come here, please. I promise I will not touch your money. Promise." He has reached the steps to the stage and comes running up. "What's your name?"

"Blake."

"Okay, please take out any bill from your wallet. Just hold it, and don't let me touch it. In fact, if I touch this bill, I want you to hit me hard in the face. In fact—if you see me touching this bill, please jump on me and choke me to death." The guy nods, laughing, looking out at his friends in the audience. "DO NOT LET ME TOUCH YOUR MONEY," I yell. He half-jumps and turns his attention back to me.

"Now, Blake, please take your bill and keep it enclosed in your hand and hold it until the end of the show. DON'T LET ME TOUCH IT. I'm also going to give you this special scroll. Please, don't unroll it, just hold on to it. Okay?" I take a large white scroll of rolled-up paper from a table on stage and hand it to Blake. He grins.

"Now listen, please go back to your seat, my friend. Every time I ask during the show, 'Where is the money?' I want you to scream, 'THE MONEY IS HERE!' and wave the bill in the air." He nods, enthusiastic now. He turns around and goes back to his seat and his friends, the bill and the scroll in his hands.

So now you've seen me perform a little. My shows are an organic process and nothing is ever fixed or static. I've performed in over forty countries around the world. Reactions to my shows are different from culture to culture—in India the audiences are reverential as if I'm a god, in Japan people get scared and run away, in Europe it's "How does he do that?" and in America people get loud with their excitement or opinions. But the one constant is the universal sense of genuine astonishment. It's an amazing feeling that we don't get to experience very often: that awareness that the things we don't know are greater than the things we do. Especially when it comes to our minds.

TWO

A Beautiful Mind

Most people, when they meet me, ask questions about my mind-reading, especially about moving objects without touching them. How do I do it? Do I have supernatural powers? During my shows, people say "wow" or "oh my god" or "awesome" a lot. People are amazed, and I like that very much. But the most amazing thing for me is this: I used to be a shy little boy with only four close friends—Yuval, Nissim, Shumer, and Yishay—but over the years, with the help of my mental skills, I turned myself into an extrovert, someone who introduces himself to total strangers and can stand on a stage and perform for anywhere from twenty to two thousand people. For me, that's the real magic. A kind of mind over matter.

I've come to understand the important role of the mind in everything I do on and off stage. Just like the people who come to my shows, I'm constantly awed by the power of our minds. Everyone's mind is capable of unbelievable things. Yours, too. We just need to understand a little about the way the mind works to harness and focus its energy and use its power.

By developing my mental abilities, I was able to become a completely different person—or at least unlock my true self. It took me a lot of reading and practice to get in front of a crowd, entertaining with my skills and positive energy. I'm not a scientist, a psychologist, or an academic. I'm not a researcher doing weird experiments in a university laboratory somewhere, but I have read psychology and business books as well as books on intuition, suggestion, guided imagination, parapsychology, even occultism. You name it, I read it. Then I went out into the world and practiced everything I'd read. I made mistakes and learned from them. Then I made completely new mistakes and learned from those, too. I gathered experience. Now I use my mind as a powerful tool in all aspects of my life, and you can, too, because I'm going to give you the key to some underground secrets. You'll learn how to use your mind's power to communicate and persuade, to make connections, to create and harness positive energy. You'll discover how to use the mind creatively to bring about change. You'll develop your intuition in such a way that you can call on it to take decisive action.

Our minds are key in everything we do. Over the next few chapters I'm going to show you some of the different ways in which I use my mind. Then I'll teach you some tricks for finding and unleashing your inner mentalist.

The first thing to remember is this: your mind is incredibly cool. Just try this experiment and see what your mind can do. It's called the Ganzfeld Procedure.

First, you'll need to halve a Ping-Pong ball and grab some tape. Next, tune a radio to a station playing static or go to Simplynoise.com to play some white noise. You can listen through head-phones if you like. Lie down and get comfortable, tape one half of the Ping-Pong ball over each eye, and relax—with your eyes open for a good few minutes.

So what happened? What did you see? Or hear? You probably saw some crazy stuff, images racing through your mind. Basically, you deprived your mind of any stimuli and when that happens it makes up its own. Interesting, right? If it can do that without any help from you, think about how amazing it can be when you learn to control it.

Before I share my cool mentalist secrets with you, let me start by explaining how I found out about my skills for the first time.

I grew up in Haifa, Israel, with my parents and two brothers, Talmor and Aviram. I was the youngest, always full of energy and very curious. We lived in a three-story house with a nice yard and deck at the back, which was good for me, because

I always liked to be on the move, exploring, imagining, climbing. The deck was very useful in a way I'm sure my parents never anticipated. I was pretty forgetful and I always forgot or lost my house keys, so I had to find creative ways of breaking into the house. Usually I'd head through the garden, up a tree, shimmy along a branch, and leap onto my bedroom window ledge. Then I'd use my metal school ruler (which somehow I never managed to lose or forget) to break the pencil that held together the window shutters, slowly open the window, and boom, there I was on my desk.

My father would close up the window and shutters again and again, but I was always able to break in. I think I'd have been a good burglar. But, luckily, I chose to be a mentalist instead. Or, to be more precise, being a mentalist chose me.

Life was always interesting with me around. I think I probably had ADHD or ADD, or one of those disorders. I used to play with everything. If I was given a toy, I would study it first, sort of research the way it looked and felt, and then I would play with it. For me this meant taking it apart to see how it worked. Even with a book, I would look at the outside, how it was made, how it felt, and feel its energy before I opened it. One day, my dad brought home a television. I took it apart the next day and couldn't put it back together. I wasn't being bad, I was just curious to find out how it worked. Luckily, my parents were quite understanding about it, but they didn't like to leave me alone with things for too long.

My parents tell me that one night when I was about six years old, I was sitting at dinner eating soup like any other boy. But then the spoon in my soup bowl started moving, just a little bit toward the edge of the bowl—without me touching it. My brothers stopped talking, my dad stared, and my mom told me to stop playing with my food. But I wasn't playing with my food—the spoon was moving. On its own. Or that's what it looked like. We all watched it shiver a little way to one side, slipping along the edge of the bowl through the soup. It was fascinating. And what was even more interesting to me was that I knew that I was making it move, that I had somehow connected with it through my mind and I was in charge. I just didn't really know how I was doing it.

It was the first time that my unusual abilities showed themselves, and from that moment I knew that I had a special skill. I just had to find out how I could control it. And my family? Well, my mom was in shock, my dad was wondering if he was drunk, and my two brothers were just waiting for me to get in trouble. My parents didn't rush me to the doctors to find out if there was something wrong with me. After all, I hadn't levitated out of my chair and across the dining room. I had maybe made a spoon move, or maybe the table had shaken or the wind had blown it—there were ways to explain it away. Easier ways than thinking your youngest son had these strange abilities.

So the incident was forgotten in the rush of everyday life and I just went back to being six years old, taking televisions apart. And thinking. I did that a lot. I was a quiet child and didn't have too many things to say—which, by the way, people now find hard to believe. I was always thinking about different ideas, taking in what other people said and thinking it through in my own way. It was my way of processing information, running it through my brain, taking it apart and storing away useful bits for later. It wasn't necessary for me to talk about my ideas, and mostly I was too shy to try, anyway, so I spent a lot of time inside my own mind. In many ways I take after my father with this. No matter what his work was, he was always coming up with ideas and plans for other things, writing them down, drawing sketches, always thinking, inventing. Like Leonardo da Vinci. It's crazy but he has drawings from ages ago for things that have only just been invented. I always joke that he could have been a billionaire by now if only he'd patented his ideas. But he's not interested. He's happy with his life.

At the time I didn't know this, but now, looking back, I'm aware I had discovered my passion. From the moment I moved that spoon a fraction of an inch across my soup bowl, my whole life started to follow one direction. Everything I did after that was about moving my life further down this track—developing my mental abilities and becoming a performer. My parents taught me to believe in my own abilities and not worry about what others thought about me. They accepted that I was a little different from the other kids.

I was still very young when I started trying out experiments on my brothers. I knew there was something going on with my mind, but I couldn't explain it. I had very strong intuition and could tell a lot about people just by looking at them, or I'd know what someone was going to say before they said it. Especially my mom. I'd ask my brothers to think of a number, and a lot of the time I guessed right. In the beginning I just tried to guess numbers between one and ten, and right away I noticed something cool. Most people say seven. There's a process of psychology. First they eliminate one and ten, because you've said "between one and ten," then they eliminate number five, because it's right in the middle. Then, for some reason, number nine goes. So that leaves only two, three, four, six, and seven. Then the majority of people will choose the number seven. Some think of it as a lucky number—it is a number that comes up a lot in various religions and in everyday life with things like seven days of the week, seven colors of the rainbow.

I became really interested in the human mind, in the way we think and act, and why. I thought about this a lot. Why did people say the number seven? Are we so predictable? I decided to see if I could make people say a different number, the number I was thinking of. And I could. I wasn't sure how I was doing it. I would look at someone and imagine a number and they would say the number. Sometimes I would concentrate on twenty-six . . . twenty-six . . . twenty-six . . . twenty-six . . . and then the person would say, "Twenty-six." Or sometimes I would just look at someone and feel a number coming from them . . . like sixty-eight. So I would say, "Sixty-eight," and it would be right about 90 percent of the time.

It was very exciting for me and incredibly rewarding, because I would get that look of amazement thrown in my direction. It made me read more and practice more. I would leave my friends and their games to go and read more and more books, anything I could get my hands on about what goes on inside people's minds. I was drawn to it and just couldn't help myself. It was so interesting to me. Not like school work at all, and I was happy to sit inside, losing myself in these books, jumping from the middle of the book to the beginning and then back again as I searched for information. This drive for knowledge came from somewhere deep within and I explored as much as I could.

At the same time I worked a lot on focusing my mind. Some people have told me that this hyper-focusing is a symptom of ADD, that you can become engrossed in something that interests you for hours, blocking out everything around you. That was definitely me when I was reading or focusing or practicing my "think of a number" routine. By the way, that's how I open all my shows now, around the world: "If I ask you to think of a number between one and one hundred, what would you say?"

I LOVE TO SEE THE SURPRISE ON PEOPLE'S FACES WHEN I DO THIS ACT. I THINK YOU WILL TOO. CHECK IT OUT ON WWW.MINDREADERBOOK.COM/THINKOFANUMBER

Once I had worked long and hard on my numbers act, I started to practice other things. I would ask my brothers to hold a small object in their hand, something like a coin or a stone, and then let me guess the hand. And I mostly guessed right. You can say that there is a fifty-fifty chance to guessing it correctly, but when you do that ten times or twenty times in a row, then it becomes something else. Around this time I was also practicing how to stop watches at a specific time and then influence someone to think of this time. My feats were getting more complex, combining different skills, building on what I had already learned.

I also started to watch people, trying to figure them out,

just like I had done with objects. I would study their faces and the way they moved, to try and work out what was going on in their minds. It was a puzzle to me, a challenge. I think I started people-watching because I was shy. I didn't say much but I observed everything and took it in and processed it. This is when I discovered something amazing. My skills became an icebreaker for me. I didn't know how to start conversations with people or even how to continue a conversation if someone else started one. There's the expression "socially awkward." That was me. But when I would try an experiment on someone, we would be engaged on a social level as if it wasn't me. It was someone else. Lior the performer. My actions were speaking for me.

The only way for me to really practice my new feats was to perform them as often as possible, so I had to start interacting with other people. It would happen like this: at school or in the neighborhood, I'd try out a routine on one of my few very close friends, they'd invite someone else over to see it, and before long there'd be a crowd of people around me. Whenever I worked with my mental skills, I'd become the center of attention. And I probably hadn't said anything to anyone other than "Do you have a watch?" or "Think of a number." In a way, I was able to hide behind my routines and observe my audience. What did they expect from me? What happened if I said something funny? I took notes in my mind. I saw that people liked my jokes and quips, that they liked to laugh, so I added this dimension. Little by little, I was developing a whole show and it all felt very natural. It was inside me all along—as my dad said, I had the gene—I just needed to let it out. So my mental skills and my showman skills grew side by side, one helping the other, as I practiced both. Sometimes I wonder: if I hadn't discovered my mental abilities, what would have happened to me? Would I still be that shy boy, observing, watching, thinking, or would my showman side have found another outlet?

Growing up, I always loved Superman, and had all the comic books, action figures, and T-shirts. He was my hero. He still is—just ask my girlfriend, Tal. She bought me a Superman ring that I never take off. The interesting thing about Superman is that he was born that way. There's a cool conversation about this superhero mythology in the movie *Kill Bill 2*. When Superman wakes up in the morning, he's Super-man. He has to change into his alter ego, Clark Kent, to fit in with the rest of the world. Think about Batman and Spider-Man—they wake up as Bruce Wayne and Peter Parker and have to change into superheroes. I've always liked this analogy, and think of it sometimes in connection with my life. As a kid, I felt like Superman when I was performing, but when I wasn't in front of a crowd, I was the other Lior, a little shy and unsure of himself. The question was, which was the real me? Which was my alter ego? Which one was I when I woke up in the morning? As I've become older and grown in self-confidence, my professional and personal lives have meshed and the lines between the two have blurred. I'll always have a soft spot for Superman.

By the age of thirteen or so, I was confident enough to put on shows for my friends at parties and bar and bat mitzvahs. We also had something in Israel where people would host shows or lectures in their living rooms for a group of thirty to fifty people. They could be anything "entertaining": an astrologist, a lecturer—me! No longer was it just a question of me running through a few of my skills in the school yard. I had a whole show now, a real performance with a real audience. I would tell them which number they were thinking about, which hand they were holding an object in, stop watches, that sort of thing. People were always impressed with the acts, but it had become important to me that they enjoy the whole experience from beginning to end, that they leave with a feeling of positive energy. My problem was that the shows were supposed to last one hour, but they couldn't get me off the stage. I always stayed longer and longer, trying out new party feats. Later, when I got a manager, he explained to me that you should always leave your audience hungry for more. The first show I ever did was for children, and I was paid 100 shekels, which is about $30. I was thirteen years old. I was so proud.

I became known as the young kid with the abilities, and I picked up quite a bit of work through people we knew. But I decided it was time to find a wider public. To do so, I needed to get my name out, which I knew could be a difficult prospect, so I set about marketing myself. I had two different approaches.

One method was to go into small restaurants and diners in Haifa and perform for free there. It takes guts to show up at a table of a big group of strangers or a couple on a date, but I would put on my best jacket, make sure my hair was combed, take a deep breath, smile, and approach. Usually I'd be very polite but confident. One of the tricks I'd learned was never to give people the chance to say no. Instead of saying, "Would you like to see something amazing?"—to which the diners could say, "No thank you," and go back to their own conversations—I'd say,

"I'm going to show you something amazing." Then I'd launch into guessing the number that they were thinking, or I'd make a spoon or a glass bend or move. The diners always responded positively. People at other tables would be turning around, seeing what the excitement was, hoping I'd go to their table next.

My appearances in restaurants had what I call the "double reality" effect. This is something I still use today. In the beginning, the owners of the restaurant would sometimes think that one of the guests had invited me, while the diners would think that the restaurant had invited me to perform. So no one asked me to leave. It works every time. I would perform for a few minutes at a few tables, entertain people, make them laugh and feel good, and then I'd leave my newly printed business cards, hoping that someone would see me and need me for an office party or a bar mitzvah. I landed some good business this way.

My other marketing technique was to send letters to various companies in Haifa that might be interested in having me put on a performance. I wanted to stand out from the crowd, so the letters and envelopes were black, and on the envelopes I printed "DO NOT OPEN THIS LETTER." Of course, the envelopes were opened—as a student of the human mind, I knew they would be—and inside there was a cheeky photograph of me with the words, "I knew you couldn't resist" and then information about my show. People like to laugh. They like to be entertained, and they appreciate a bit of good-humored mischief in the middle of the day. I received a lot of phone calls from those letters I sent out.

Sometimes I used my growing abilities to win over my teachers at school. By the time I entered high school, I had stopped being outwardly shy. Suddenly I had a lot to say in class about a lot of things. My best subjects were the sciences and math—subjects with concrete answers—and for those I received a stream of constant As. My B subjects were the abstract ones, like Bible, literature, and history. My answers were never what the teachers wanted to hear. A teacher might say the poet wrote those lines because he was feeling platonic love for his mother, but I would always disagree and offer a different interpretation—one that the teacher would interpret as a B. However, I managed to raise my grade in my Bible class because I guessed which exact word my teacher would point to in the Bible, and my gym teacher gave me a higher grade because I predicted the outcome of a school basketball game. Those abilities were definitely useful to have. Fifteen years later, I'm still using those skills. Look at this quote from the *New York Post,* July 29, 2011: "During Major League Soccer's All-Star Game at Red Bull Arena on Wednesday night, mentalist Lior Suchard entertained with his mind-blowing tricks. Before the match Suchard correctly predicted the halftime score as well as which players would score goals and when." Sound familiar?

My favorite teacher was my math teacher. I really respected him, as he found a way to guarantee my cooperation. At the end of every lesson he would give me a few minutes to perform in front of the class—as long as my performance included math. In exchange he expected me not to interrupt during his class. I had great fun with his proposal and it helped me focus on the idea of performing something new each day for an audience. In this way I stretched and tested my abilities. So what kind of feats did I do to entertain my math class? I would write down a number on a piece of paper and keep that number secret. Then I would ask the teacher to come up with a mathematical formula. Any formula. No matter which formula he chose, the answer would always be the number written on the paper. It was great fun to see his surprise every time. I used to push the limit. I'd write a number on a piece of paper and give it to him in an envelope and say, "Think of a number. But don't tell me yet. And, by the way, don't open the envelope." After a few days I'd ask if he'd thought of a number. Finally he'd say yes and then open the envelope. Of course, the number he'd thought of was the number on the piece of paper. He'd be blown away each time, because he'd always have thought of two or three numbers then changed his mind and still the number he settled on would be the one in the envelope. I also used to play a game where I'd write out a formula on a piece of paper that only I would see. Then the teacher would come up with a number. His number would be the answer to my formula. Every single time.

By the way, speaking of math, here's an easy riddle for you. If chocolate and chewing gum cost $1.10 together and the chocolate costs $1.00 more than the gum, how much does the gum cost?

You're probably thinking 10 cents, right? Way to go. Except you're wrong. The answer is 5 cents. Later on you'll find out why you're not the only one to get this riddle wrong.

Recently I went back to visit my math teacher and he told me something very interesting. He's been a teacher for over forty years and has taught many, many kids during that time. But he's only seen a very small percentage of kids come through his classroom door who've known exactly what they wanted to do with their lives. I was one of them. He knew when I was in high school that it wouldn't matter what grades I got, which school I attended, or which subjects I studied. The end result would be the same, because I had a passion and a dream. I was aiming for something. It was very exciting for me to hear him say that.

After high school I signed up for the IDF, the Israel Defense Forces. It's mandatory in Israel, for three years. You're away from home and expected to take responsibility—and so you become responsible. It's a very good experience. I managed to keep performing during my time there, doing unofficial shows as a combat soldier. I also had other duties that used my mental abilities, which I can't talk about—otherwise, you know, I'd have to kill you. And then, when I came out of the army, I set about achieving my goals of becoming the best mentalist in the world.

I got myself a manager, and together we worked incredibly hard finding shows for me. I performed everywhere I could, no matter how small the event, even performing free of charge. I wanted to get my name out there. I worked the entertainment circuit in Israel—bar mitzvahs, private parties, corporate parties—and, little by little, more work, in different countries, started to come in. I didn't say no to anything. I worked like crazy.

One night I was invited to a private party in Israel to perform before a crowd of people. There was nothing unusual about the event—I had done many other such parties—but at this one I was asked a question that made a big difference in my life.

The host of the party owned a large telecommunications company and he was about to launch a new cell phone. This was a big new product for him, and he was hoping it would make a huge splash in the cell phone world. Toward the end of the party, he approached me and told me about this high-quality, next-generation cell phone. Then, to my surprise, he asked if I would be able to go to an international trade show and help with the marketing. My first thought was that I had never done anything like this before and had no idea of what was expected or whether I could do what he was hoping for. So, of course, I said yes, absolutely, I would be very happy to be involved. Then, when I arrived home that evening, I thought, what have I got myself into? I had all kinds of worries. What if this new role took me away from the live performances and television shows that I hoped would be the direction of my career? Was this selling out? What if I truly couldn't find a way to promote a cell phone? I'd only ever done entertainment, not product pitches.

I fought down the panic in my stomach and rephrased the question "How the hell am I going to do this?" into "What is the best possible way I can prepare for this event?" Then I added another question, "How can I make this trade show part of my career path?"

After that, I learned everything I could about the telecommunications business, the company I was working with, and their competition. I read books and articles on marketing and sales. I even made a special trip to an overseas trade conference to see exactly what takes place and what would be expected of me.

Finally, the day of the event came around. The stage was set. Me in front of two thousand people. One of my biggest shows ever. After some preliminary banter, I invited ten randomly selected people up onto the stage with their cell phones. One by one, I asked them to call home or to call a friend. Most of them failed to do so. Their calls wouldn't go through—no reception, they said. A few were able to make their calls successfully and I gathered them together at the edge of the stage. "Which cell phone are you using?" I asked them all, one by one. And, of course, the successful cell phones were made by the company I was promoting. The huge audience was very impressed and applauded wildly. I didn't have to add other words to the sales pitch: the message was received loud and clear.

Since that first trade show, I have performed at dozens of others all over the world. My solution is always to create a metaphor for the clients so that their product will be remembered. For Hewlett-Packard laser printers, I came up with the concept of mind-printing instead of mind-reading. For BMW, I drove a silver E250 blindfolded, the slogan "You can count on BMW with your eyes closed" emblazoned on giant screens. I interlace my abilities with the products.

I ALSO HAD A LOT OF FUN DRIVING BLINDFOLDED IN MY FRIEND'S PORSCHE. YOU CAN SEE HOW NERVOUS HE WAS AT **WWW.MINDREADERBOOK.COM/PORSCHE**

One day a few years ago, I received a phone call from a producer at a TV show. They had heard of me through the infotainment business. They wanted me to appear as a contestant on a new reality TV show called *The Successor,* which would be broadcast in Israel and a bunch of other countries around the world, hosted by Uri Geller, celebrated Israeli mystifier and entertainer. The idea behind the show was for Uri to choose the next great mentalist, his so-called successor. Uri has been internationally famous since the 1970s for his amazing mental abilities such as bending spoons, stopping clocks on command, and using incredible telepathic skills. He has advised celebrities and business leaders around the globe, has helped companies find oil, and was the first true infotainer. He's also famous for the number of skeptics who devote so much of their time to trying to prove he is a fake. I accepted immediately.

There were nine different mentalists in the running, competing to win the title, and over a twelve-week period we all used our mental skills to perform mind-bending, mesmerizing acts hoping to win the favor of Uri, the judges, the studio audience, and viewers at home who could also vote. It was an amazing experience and great fun. All the mentalists knew each other, so there was a huge amount of laughter and positive energy.

I learned so much from being on live TV. The added pressure of being followed around by cameras wasn't really so different from performing in front of an audience at a party. You always have to be on your toes as a mentalist, as a performer. You have to be ready to ad lib and be spontaneous, change your act if necessary. It was interesting to think about the television viewers watching the performances in their homes. It forced me to think about keeping the performance personal for the live audience, but also to focus on being charismatic enough to amaze people you can't even see.

On the final show, I was announced as the winner. The successor. Two-thirds of the voters voted for me. Uri Geller even said, "I've stopped the clock Big Ben twice but what you did impressed me more." This was a great moment in my life. I became a bit of a celebrity in Israel and Europe, especially Israel. By being on TV I had performed inside many people's living rooms and suddenly I couldn't step outside without wearing sunglasses. It was exciting.

Many people think of *The Successor* as my big break, but I don't really view it like that. It made all the hard work I'd been doing for the past few years more public. The media attention that came with winning was fun for a while and it got me more phone calls and more work, but after it was over, I just went back to what I was doing before—working very hard to become the best mentalist in the world.

THREE

The Power of the Mind—You Think, Therefore I Am

I ask Amy to think of a person, male or female, that there's no way that I could know. Someone who's not at the meeting, in the conference room at my publisher's office. There's a bunch of us in here, and all eyes are on Amy. She nods briefly. She seems quiet but confident. Immediately, she thinks of a person. I can tell by the concentration on her face that her decision is made, that she's not wavering and changing her mind. "It's a woman," I say. She nods and smiles. I look carefully at her face, at her eyes, moving quite close to her. "There are five letters in her name." Again, a nod, a smile. She is empathetic, wanting me to succeed. Her mind is very open—it makes it much easier for me. "Does anyone in this room know her?" She shakes her head. I'm holding a pen and card in my hands and I start to write. I'm seeing letters now, an image. I start to write the letters down. An *N*, an *I*. "She's very close to you?" I say. It's not really a question. I know she is by the strength of Amy's thoughts. I'm done with my writing now—I have a five-letter word, a name, written down on the card. I show it around the room but make sure that Amy cannot see. TANIA. Everyone looks first at the card, then over at Amy, people in the second row craning to see her face. They want to know the name. "So, Amy," I ask. "What was the name you thought of?" A moment's pause—she has good timing. "Tania," she says. Everyone gasps. I show her the card. "She's my best friend," says Amy. "And that's exactly how she spells her name. With an *I* not a *Y*." Which makes sense, because that's how she thought about the name when she thought of her friend, and that's the way I saw the name in her mind. Everyone is excited, talking now. How did I do it? How could I have gone inside Amy's mind and pulled out this name?

I've read thousands of people's minds and pulled out thousands of names of friends, first loves, first teachers. I love to read minds. It shows the essence of what I do and the power of the mind so clearly. One mind going into another. It's cool, and it makes people stop for a moment to think about how amazing the mind really is. Not only my mind, but Amy's, too. She was able to conjure up an image of her friend inside her mind when that friend was far away. That's a very complex process. Not only that but she was able to hold this image in her mind for quite a long time while responding to questions I asked her. And, probably, she had a million other thoughts whirring through her mind at the same time: What if Lior doesn't guess correctly? I wonder what Tania's doing right now. What if Lior can read everything in my mind? And what's really cool is that everyone in that room could have done the same thing.

Take reading this book, for example. Just seeing the symbols that make up words sets in process a whole whirlwind of activity in your brain. That's before you've even translated the symbols into words and sentences with meaning, which, in turn, will spark other connections in your brain as you engage your intellect and your emotions. Not to mention you're also registering the sound of traffic in the street, remembering that it's your brother's birthday, noting that you're thirsty, and figuring out that it's probably time to go to work soon. All in the time it took you to read that sentence. The mind is an incredible thing.

We all know that we have five senses: sight, smell, taste, touch, and hearing. I can still remember learning about it as a kid. Our senses let us process and perceive the world around us. Guess what? It's not that simple. Scientists now agree that we have other senses, too, other ways of taking in outside information. You know how you ride a bicycle? Through your sense of balance. And what tells you to wear gloves on a freezing cold day? That would be your sense of temperature. It also tells you to stop touching the hot iron. I used this one a lot when I was a kid. We also have senses that help to detect pain or tell us how heavy something is. And then there are senses of time and direction—although I know many people who don't seem to have either one.

For me, there's another sense, too, that is very, very interesting. It is what is commonly known as the "sixth sense." What do I mean by this? It means perceiving the world through my mind, using this sense in addition to the other senses to see and understand things in a special way. I believe that through our attention we create fields of perception that stretch out around us. Some of us are more sensitive to those fields or we are able to focus our attention more intensely. People ask me all the time whether I have supernatural powers—I don't. Even though I use the word "supernatural" in my show, I don't believe that my skills are unnatural in any way. I don't say that I'm psychic or clairvoyant. Instead I say that I have certain "skills" or "abilities" and I believe that everyone has them. To some degree. We all use our minds differently. For me, it was a question of discovering as a young kid that I had this talent for using my mind in a different way, and then deciding to practice and hone this skill. It was all about focusing, and I mean really, really, really focusing on the matter. You can't just want a spoon to bend or move. Or to read someone's thoughts. You have to focus and practice. And, as you know, I practiced a lot.

There's a famous moment when South African golfer Gary Player hit a perfect shot three hundred yards into the hole. Appreciation and wonder rippled through the crowd, and one spectator called out, "Lucky shot!" To which Gary responded, "You're right. But the funny thing is, the harder I practice, the luckier I get."

How to Focus on Focusing

Focusing the mind is about emptying it of distractions so that we can think clearly. Kids find it easier to get into deep concentration because they live in the moment and don't worry about things that aren't in the here and now. Adults, on the other hand, are often not fully present because they are distracted—and don't realize it. Learn to ask yourself, "What's on my mind right now?" Maybe you're thinking about a phone call you have to make and it's stopping you from focusing. If you can, handle distractions immediately. Or put them on a list to handle later, so your mind can relax for now and you can use all your brain power for the task at hand.

There's a blind artist, John Bramblitt, who, after losing his sight, learned to paint by feeling the different textures of different-color paints. He sees so well through touch that he paints portraits that are exactly lifelike—of people he's never seen in his life before. How amazing is that? There are blind people who can ride mountain bikes and navigate pathways through forests because they've learned the skill of echolocation to get around. There are deaf composers who create the most beautiful symphonies but never hear that music played aloud. There are so many ways of perceiving the world. Why is it so surprising then that someone can read minds or use mental energy to bend silverware?

The mind is an amazing thing.

My show is called *Supernatural Entertainment*. The name is self-explanatory. The show delves into the supernatural, into those areas beyond the five senses that deal with extrasensory perception. And, equally important, it is pure entertainment. My aim is to provide a positive, thrilling experience for the audience each time I perform.

I've described the way I use my thoughts as similar to working with a laser beam compared to a flashlight. When I play basketball, I'm definitely a flashlight to Michael Jordan's laser beam. Or playing the guitar? Well, I'm better than a flashlight but no laser beam. We could go on here, but you get the picture. I'm sure you have many talents where you're closer to a laser beam, and others—well, we can just forget about those.

Here are some things I can do with my mind:

- Know a number you're thinking of between one and one hundred
- Know your first love's name
- Know your first teacher's name
- Know your birth sign and birth date
- Know the name you've thought of for your unborn child
- Bend a coin or spoon or nail in your hand
- Bend the stem of a wine glass
- Make your eyeglasses jump into the air
- Tell you a story that only you would know
- Transfer energy between you and another person
- Make you think you're being touched when you're not
- Predict which word you will choose in a book that you randomly choose from hundreds
- Predict numbers now that you will say when I ask you tomorrow

- Mess up a baseball player's swing

- Win in any poker game

Here are some things I cannot do:

- Guess the lottery—as it is figured out by machines (although I've come close)

- Read the thoughts of random strangers walking along

- Read all your thoughts as I sit across from you at dinner

- Find missing persons—although I wish I could

- Cure diseases (I've been asked many times)

- Speak to the dead (actually, I can speak to the dead—they just never answer me!)

- Walk along sidewalks without falling into holes

- Gain weight even though I try

- Play casinos in Vegas

I use different aspects of my mental skills for each of the different feats I do and combine them with techniques I've picked up from psychology along the way. For mind-reading, I'll read the overall person as well as the mind, using clues like body language and eye movement to help me channel my thought processes, and to focus more clearly on the exact name or image the person is thinking about.

Whenever I give you a choice to think of something,

whether it's a number between one and one hundred, or a word in a book chosen from hundreds of books on a shelf, I'll write down ahead of time what your choice will be. This seems like I'm making a prediction. And, in a way, I am making a prediction, but it's one that is called an open prediction. The question is, "Is it possible to read a mind when the thought isn't there yet?" Wrap your mind around that one for a moment. How can I predict a number when you haven't thought of it yet? It's the same for the word. How can I predict which word you'll choose when you haven't even selected a book to choose it from yet? But the reality is that you choose a number or a word because I make you do so. I persuade you. I influence you. I zip into your thought process and plant that word or that number. How cool is that?

London, 2009

Sometimes I'll do a little mind-reading and a little persuasion at the same time. The lines blur. I'm at an office party in an old converted warehouse near the river. I ask Penny to go outside the room and think of a time in her mind. Any time, whatever time she wants. While she's gone, I ask a young guy, Peter, to turn the dial on his watch, making the hands spin backward and forward, backward and forward, and to stop whenever he wants. All while hiding the face of the watch so no one, including Peter, can see the time.

Next I call Penny back into the room. "Did you think of a time?" I ask her. "Yes," she says. "Does the time have a specific meaning for you, or is it just a random time?" "It's special," she says, nodding enthusiastically. Next I ask her to visualize the time on a clock. "Imagine Big Ben, or just a big clock." In this way, she sees the time in her mind as analog and not digital. It's easier for me to feel it this way. At that point, the image of the time becomes very clear to me. I write it down on my card, keeping it hidden. I look over at Penny. Her face is alive with emotion. "Please say the time you were thinking about." "Seven fifty-five," she says. "It's the time I was born." "That's amazing, because I wrote down on my card '7:55,'" I say, showing everyone the card. Penny gasps. She can't believe it.

"That's crazy," says someone a few rows away. Everyone in the room is moved that I read Penny's mind and found such a personal time in there.

"But wait," I say. "There's more. You remember that Peter turned the hands on his watch and chose when to stop? And no one saw the time?" Everyone is nodding, anticipating. "Well, Peter, could you please look at your watch and tell us the time."

He holds up the watch. "Seven fifty-five," he says. He's

shaking his head, astonished. "Incredible," someone shouts. Everyone bursts into applause.

Amazing, right? But there's another layer to this. Here's my question to you. Did I read Penny's mind while she was outside the room and get the watch to stop at the same time? Or did I stop the watch at 7:55 first and then persuade Penny to think of that time? And, if I persuaded her, how did I know to persuade her to think of a time that had such emotional meaning to her? The time of her birth? Coincidence? I don't think so. I don't believe in coincidences. Mind-boggling, yes. I've done this kind of thing many times, when I ask people to think of a number. I'll plant a number in their mind and then they'll tell me they thought of that number because it has special associations for them. One woman told me she'd thought of the number ninety-one because her grandfather had just turned ninety-one. In reality, I had written down that number before even asking her to think of a number. It makes you think, right?

I mentioned earlier another aspect of my mental skill—the transfer of positive energy, or chi energy. It's essentially a form of vital energy that unites body, mind, and spirit, that I create and control using my mind. It involves extreme focus of my thoughts to gather and send energy—enough energy to make eyeglasses fly through the air, to bend spoons and coins in someone's hand, or to stop a watch. Or even to transfer energy from one person to another. This kind of mentalism is really interesting, because it's where my thoughts can clearly be seen to operate outside my mind, projecting beyond my body, showing themselves in a physical way. It's mind over matter, of the purest kind.

So, mind-reading, persuasion, and chi energy are the elements of how I use my mind as a mentalist. It's the basic answer to "how do you do that?" It's all about harnessing the power of the mind in very specific ways. I'll talk in more depth about what I do in later chapters, and open a door to a world of underground secrets that you can use. I really believe that everyone can increase their mental powers—maybe not to the point of being a mentalist but enough to move a little way along the road from flashlight to laser beam.

You've probably guessed that I love everything to do with the mind and how it works. I consider it part of my job to read everything I can about the mechanisms of our brains, about our thought processes, about how we think the way we do.

Mind over matter is a really interesting concept, especially when we think of it in terms of metal-bending and objects flying through the air. But what if I were to tell you that we all use it all the time? Think about the placebo effect for a moment. We've all heard of medical studies in which patients are given a treatment that, in reality, does not affect them physically in any way and absolutely cannot cure them. But the important point is that the patient is told that the treatment will help their medical condition, and so they believe that it will. In this case, the mind takes over. It gets to work in helping the body to heal. Mind over matter.

There was a study in Germany, where people were spun around quickly in a motorized chair. Before the ride, some of them were given a licorice-flavored wafer to chew and told, "This helps to prevent nausea." When asked how they felt after the ride, they all felt much, much better than the ones who didn't receive the special medicine. The licorice-flavored wafer was just candy, but as soon as their minds received the information that they were being given a medication, their brains sent out signals that set in motion the body's own pain relievers. So they didn't feel nausea. Cool, right?

If I tell you that you're going to have a great day, then you will, simply because your mind will process this information and internalize this expectation. If I tell you that you're going to have the worst day of your life, then, believe me, you will. You'll be caught in the rain without an umbrella, show up late for a meeting, lose the client you've been hoping to win—to your archenemy—get dumped by your boyfriend or girlfriend. And that's just before lunch. You get the picture. And not just because I'm a mind-reader and persuading you that it's true. It's the Pygmalion effect, a self-fulfilling prophecy, a prediction that causes itself to be true—and there's even scientific data to back it up.

In an informal study, a teacher divided her class of nine-year-olds into two groups, according to eye color, and told one group that they were superior in intelligence and more likely to succeed. They were allowed special privileges and were spoken to in a positive way, compared to the inferior group. The superior group did much better on their school work that day, while the inferior group performed very badly. A few days later, the groups were reversed. In that day's math and spelling tests, the new superior group (the former inferior group) did very well and the new inferior group (the former superior group) did very badly— merely based on suggestion and the mind's processing of that suggestion.

Getting Sneaky with the Subconscious

Our minds are at work without our knowing it, from the moment we wake in the morning and start making our multitasking way through our world. We've learned all kinds of shortcuts and automatic responses for dealing with the things we don't need to think about—those little details like breathing, or knowing, by the smell coming from the kitchen, the first cup of coffee is ready—so that we can focus our minds on the morning commute or navigating the treadmill at the gym. All the time we're viewing the world through our senses and acting and reacting to the external stuff, while focusing on the internal stuff—what did your girlfriend mean last night when she said she was working late? What's the name of that new movie you want to see? Our conscious minds are busy, busy, busy. And then there's the subconscious. Most of the time we're not even aware of our subconscious, but it makes up a great percentage of our mental processes. It, too, is active even if we're not always sure of what it's doing.

Would you like to start off by playing a game with me so we can get into the world of your subconscious mind? I want you to think of two simple geometric shapes, one inside the other, but don't tell me yet. First read my advice to you very carefully. Ready?

Choosing is such a personal matter.
I want you to sit down and
Relax for a moment and
Calmly think about your options.
Let yourself breathe deeply, in and out, and
Enable your mind to go blank and focused

Imagine an empty canvas in your mind.
Now I want you to think about two simple geometric
Shapes. They are one
Inside the other in the
Deep recesses of your mind.
Empty your mind of everything else.

Think about those shapes
Rippling through your mind one
Inside the other
And visualize them
Noting their
Geometric
Lines and their strong
Energy

Now hold the shapes in your mind. Which ones did you think of?

If you're like 80 percent of people—and open to some subtle subliminal persuasion—you will have imagined this . . . turn the page:

Now look back at the first letter of each sentence of my advice. Interesting, right? And if you didn't choose this combination of shapes, don't worry. Just know that I won't be playing poker with you any time soon!

Here's another way of seeing your subconscious at work. Imagine that, by some miracle, you're running ahead of schedule and you have time this morning to pop into a grocery store before heading off to work. You decide to buy a cereal, and head over to the cereal aisle, where dozens of different boxes and packages shout their brands and logos from the shelves. You scan the rows and see a product that you've never tried before but you're sure is delicious. And even healthy, too. Crunchy ChocoNuts. You don't know why you want it but it seems like the right choice, even a familiar choice. So you buy the cereal and head down the stairs into the subway station. Usually you race down these concrete stairs, eyes and ears straining for signs of an arriving train. But this morning, you're early. So you stroll down the steps not worrying about the train, and taking in details that you wouldn't usually register: the broken tile on the wall ahead, the new blue paint on the ticket booth, and an advertising poster right in front of you for Crunchy ChocoNuts. Delicious—and even healthy, too. You've never seen this poster before in the mad rush of your mornings. But your subconscious mind has registered it and acted upon it—without your own knowledge. The box of Crunchy ChocoNuts in your bag bears witness to this. This is why advertisers fight with each other to bombard our minds with subliminal messages.

People have asked me if I use subliminal messages in my acts to help with mind-reading. Like maybe putting the number thirty-eight on the back of each seat in the auditorium at my performances and then asking someone to think of a number between one and one hundred—and they guess thirty-eight. But that's not really the way I use the power of my thoughts. I've honed my skills to the point where I work in a very subtle, subliminal way, but it can't really be rationalized or pinpointed like the ChocoNuts poster. Now, if I did put the number thirty-eight on everyone's seat, could I influence someone NOT to say it? That's a more interesting question to me.

Putting Your Mind in Gear

So what else can our amazing brains do? Take a look at the following sentence:

> *Aoccdrnig to rscheearch at Cmabrigde Uinervtisy, it deosn't mttaer in waht oredr the ltteers in a wrod are, the olny*

iprmoetnt tihng is taht the frist and lsat ltteer be at the rghit pclae. The rset can be a toatl mses and you can sitll raed it wouthit porbelm. Tihs is bcuseae the huamn mnid deos not raed ervey lteter by istlef, but the wrod as a wlohe.

You probably didn't have any problems in reading it. While it turns out that the information provided here is not entirely accurate (and you can read the whole story at http://www.mrc-cbu.cam.ac.uk/people/matt.davis/Cambrigde/) what strikes me is that it is cool that the mind can decipher these words at all. Our brains can make sense of nonsense. They like to put a logical spin on things.

Are you up for a challenge? See if you have the brain power to read the following text that I received as an e-mail. You'll probably find it gets easier the farther you read.

F1gur471v31y 5p34k1ng

7H15 M3554G3 53RV35 70 PR0V3
HOW OUR M1ND5 C4N DO 4M4Z1NG
    7H1NG5!
1MPR3551V3 7H1NGS!
1N 7H3 B3G1NN1NG 17 WA5 H4RD BU7
NOW, ON 7H15 LIN3 YOUR M1ND 1S
R34D1NG 17 4U70M471C4LLY
W17HOU7 3V3N 7H1NK1NG 4BOU7 17.
B3 H4PPY, ONLY C3R741N P30PL3 C4N
    R3AD 7H15!

A lot of the time our minds take mental shortcuts so they don't have to wade through and process every single bit of information that is thrown at them. We take in information and, based on what we already know from our life experience, we come to conclusions. Most of the time, this works out just fine. If we see a four-legged piece of furniture at a table, we know this is a chair and we don't need to analyze every nail or the grain of the wood to know this is true. We glance and our brain fills in the rest. We move on with our lives. But sometimes our brain takes a shortcut that leads us in the wrong direction completely, with surprising results.

Hold that thought and let me read your mind for a minute. Turn to the color insert in the center of the book.

Now take a look at this sentence:

WONDERS OF PERCEPTION

It's easy for us to read, right? Wonders of perception. Our brain is able to fill in the blanks, based on our knowledge and past experience, and come up with the rest of the words. Pretty impressive.

Except that it's wrong. This particular shortcut has not served us well. Here are the words.

WQNDFBS QE PFBCFPTLQN

Here's another one:

Say this sentence out loud. Now say it again. Now say it really slowly so that you pause after every single word. Aha! Now you see that you missed the second "the" the first time around, because your brain sensed familiarity and slipped into autopilot. Amazing what you can miss, isn't it?

Now count the number of *F*s in this sentence.

> *Finished files are the result*
> *of years of scientific study*
> *combined with the experience*
> *of years . . .*

How did you do? Did you get three or four? Would you believe me if I told you that there are six Fs? Try again. It can take some people three or four readings to catch all of them.

Our brain doesn't register the word "of" with its letter "f," because it is such a common word. We just zip right past it, our brains on autopilot.

So you see that reality can play tricks on our minds, making us take a step back and say, hold on. Let me engage my brain and think this time. This time, focus your brain first and see if you can read this sentence:

I love Paris in the the springtime.

While it seems that our minds can get things wrong a lot of the time, the fact is that there's a crazy amount of stuff going on inside our brains, and so we have to rely on these shortcuts. We don't have time to analyze and double-check every single tiny piece of information that comes our way. Most of the time, these shortcuts work. But, sometimes, we need to be more mindful, more aware of what's going on, and less ready to fall back onto autopilot in our lives. We need to tell our minds who's in charge.

I have to do this a lot as a mentalist. I need to make my mind work for me in ways that I can control. To take that power and manipulate it, whether it's through channeling chi energy, using intuition, focus, influence, and persuasion, or reading body language and nonverbal expressions. These all increase our control of our minds and unleash its power.

Here's a funny way of showing how you can focus your thoughts to stop your mind from running on autopilot.

Start circling your right foot clockwise—to the right, and keep drawing circles with it. Now use your finger to draw a number six in the air. What happens to your foot? If you're like most people, your foot will automatically start circling counter-clockwise—to the left. Try it again, this time trying to will your foot to circle to the right. It's hard, but it can be done. It's like mind over mind over matter! You're fighting your mind's own natural inclination to follow the movement and direction of your hand. The more you focus on it, the easier it will become.

Here's a Necker Cube, an image that our brains interpret as a 3-D image. In reality, it's just twelve intersecting lines, but most people see it as a cube with the lower left face as the front. It is possible to make the image shift. Sometimes this will happen spontaneously, but you can also do it purposely.

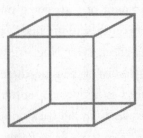

Focus your mind to pull the back face of the left-facing cube up to the right so that it becomes the top face of a right-facing cube. Try it—it's fun to manipulate the image—and to see that what our eyes see is only the version that our mind enables us to see.

As you have just seen, the most important lesson for using the full power of your mind is to first be aware of it in all its complexity. Acknowledge that your mind is amazing. Then be aware of how often we switch from active thinking to speeding along on autopilot. How often do you walk somewhere and realize you have no memory of the journey because your thoughts have been elsewhere? Of course, sometimes it's fine to be on autopilot, but most of us do it more than we should. You need to consciously put your mind into gear and use it, especially if you want something from other people. As you'll see.

Las Vegas, 2011

900 People

Now back to the show. Up until now, I've guessed a number, guessed a name, and Blake is holding on to a scroll and a $5 bill, and no one's touching the money.

I've invited a woman, Jane, up onto the stage to help me. She's a little nervous. "Jane," I say and I place my hand gently on her shoulder. "Do we know each other personally?"

"No," she says, shaking her head vigorously.

"You seem to be very happy about this. Why?" Now she's laughing, relaxing a little.

"I need your help in finding a phone number." I hand her a huge local phone book and she staggers under the weight of it. "I'd like you to choose any phone number in the whole book. Any at all from the hundreds of thousands of numbers inside. Your choice." Jane quickly riffles through the book, her eyes searching everywhere. "Take your time," I say. "Because while you're searching for a number we're going to have some fun."

I step lightly down into the audience with some big white cards. Each card has a number on it. There's a real positive energy down here. "Okay," I say, stopping by the front row next to a group of women in their twenties. "I choose all of you." They giggle. "I'm going to hand you these cards and you're going to shuffle them up between you, mix, mix, mix, just like musical chairs so we'll have a completely random combination of numbers. And stop whenever you want to. Okay?" They nod enthusiastically and I hand over the cards. Already they're passing them back and forth. The music plays.

"Jane, have you chosen yet?" Up on stage, Jane nods, and I address the row of women with the cards. "Remember, when you're ready, stop mixing the cards." There's some last-minute movement, one card passed along to the very end of the row, laughter from the women, and then they stop. "Keep them face-down until I tell you, okay? So no one can see the numbers." They all clasp the cards as if their lives depend on it, smiling, waiting. I run back up the steps to the stage.

"So Jane, just to make sure it's fair. Did I tell you which number to choose?"

Jane laughs and shakes her head.

"So tell us then which number you chose out of the whole phone book."

I take a marker and stand by the flip chart, ready to write. "464-9672," says Jane.

I repeat the numbers, "4 6 4 9 6 7 2," pausing after each one and writing it big so that everyone in the room can see.

"Thank you, Jane." Now I look out into the audience. "So, out of about a half million numbers in this phone book, Jane chose a random but specific number. 464-9672." I point to the number on the flip chart. "Now, it's impossible to predict the number chosen by Jane and it's impossible to predict the random combination of numbers created by the women in the front row. So what is the chance that one would match the other?

"Now, ladies." I look down into the audience at the row where the card shufflers sit. "Please stand up one by one, starting from this end, turn around and hold up the cards one by one so everyone can see the numbers." The first woman stands and holds up her card: 4. Then the next woman holds up a 6. People in the audience are craning their necks, whispering to each other. The following number is a 4. The audience is getting louder. "No way!" shouts someone in the back. The women with the numbers are laughing, shaking their heads. Now the remaining women, in turn, show their numbers: 9, 6, 7. People in the audience are shouting out the numbers now. There's tension in the air. Electricity. The woman with the final card holds it to her chest, nervous to show it. "On three," I shout and the audience counts down with me, "Three, two, one." She turns the card; it's a 2. The audience erupts into a cheer, leaping out of their seats. We're all laughing. It's amazing. The energy is crazy.

Suddenly I yell out, "I haven't forgotten. Where is the money?"

At the back of the room, Blake leaps out of his seat, clutching the bill and the scroll. "THE MONEY IS HERE." Everyone laughs even harder.

FOUR

The Power of Persuasion—Great Minds Think Alike

I'm on a big talk show in Japan, and the stage is filled with newspapers. Dozens and dozens of Japanese newspapers, over four hundred of them, stacked in overflowing piles. Professor Ootsuki is a well-known professor in Japan, and he's a skeptic. A huge skeptic. I'm going to change his mind by predicting which single word the TV host, Takeshi Kitano, will choose from all the newspapers. I hope. Did I mention that all the newspapers are in Japanese? I don't speak Japanese.

The professor watches closely as I look at the mountain of newspapers, and then as I look at the host, searching her face. He isn't smiling but he's curious, I can tell. I write a word on a big piece of white paper—so only I can see. I'm writing Japanese symbols. I have no idea what the word means or how to pronounce it, just that this is the word that will be chosen. Next I fold up the paper and place it in an envelope. Then I give the envelope to the professor, who signs his name on it and keeps a tight hold of it.

With preparations done, and my prediction made, I have just one job left to do. That is to influence the host to choose this one word from all the tens of thousands of words scattered on the ground before her. I explain that she has a series of choices to make. First, she needs to choose a newspaper. She takes a little time with this but then she takes one, pulling it deep from the pile. Next, she must choose the left-hand page or right-hand page of her newspaper. She does that quickly—the right page. Then it's time to choose her word. When she has chosen, she smiles and quickly goes to write her word on a big whiteboard so that everyone—including the professor and me—can see. She writes: **ホテル**.

With great flourish and drum roll, we get the professor to open the envelope, signed by him and still in his hand. He pulls out the piece of paper on which I have predicted the word, unfolds it carefully, and holds it up for everyone to see. It is the exact same word: **ホテル**. The host and studio audience go wild. They tell me that this means "hotel." I predicted that the host would choose this specific word out of all the words available to her, and she did. The professor just sits there nodding. He is very, very shocked. And maybe not a skeptic anymore. I was so excited by this routine that I did it again live on *The Tonight Show with Jay Leno*. And Kim Kardashian. But with an interesting twist that I'll tell you about later . . .

CHECK OUT THIS AMAZING FEAT AT
WWW.MINDREADERBOOK.COM/JAPAN

Remember that I call this kind of prediction an "open prediction," as I'm predicting something that hasn't happened yet. How does this work? I'm not reading the future, because I can't do that. Instead I'm influencing the future. I'm causing it to bend to my wishes by persuading the host to choose the word that I predicted. Cool, right? But that's not all. It's possible to persuade more than one person at a time.

Imagine that you're sitting in the audience at one of my shows. I come bounding down to your section of the audience and ask you and the people sitting around you to all think of a number. Your number is forty-four. Everyone's number is forty-four. And, of course, I know that you're all thinking of the number forty-four. I ask all of you a general question: am I reading your minds or am I influencing you to think of a certain number? At first, most people say that they think I'm reading minds. But I can see they're not sure. They haven't really thought about the possibility that I could be persuading them. It's an interesting question. I ask everyone to again think of a number. And guess what? Everyone thinks of the number thirty-seven. Including you. How can that be? How can everyone have thought of the exact same number? You're pretty amazed, sitting there in the audience. So now what do you think—am I reading your mind or persuading you to think of a number? It really gets people thinking—and talking—about the power of the mind.

Every time I go up to someone and say, "Think of a number between one and a hundred," I am being persuasive. In my shows, I'll first write down a number on a whiteboard, and then I'll ask the person to think of a number. When they say their number out loud, I show them the board—with that number written on it. The person is always amazed. Very often they will tell me that they thought of several different numbers before they settled on their final number—or I'll tell them that they did. A lot of people think of a number with a seven in it first, and then decide to change it. Or they'll think of a number that they consider too easy for me to guess and they'll change it. But the reality is that I am influencing them to think of a certain number. I interrupt their thought process, and tell them what to say. This is the power of persuasion.

I know you're thinking, that's really cool, but how? How do you do it? Well, part of my answer is that to this day I do not know all the reasons. It is something that I have spent years developing and it comes naturally to me, so it is difficult to take it all apart and analyze it step-by-step. However, I have studied, and read, and practiced everything I possibly could about the psychology of persuasion and I've developed some methods in this way.

One of the areas I'm especially interested in is Neuro-linguistic Programming (NLP), and it's a very important part of what I do. It explores the relationship between how we think and how we communicate, both verbally and nonverbally. For example, if I raise my hand as if I'm going to punch you, you will automatically shield your face. Everything we do in life triggers something else. Everything we do causes a response in another person. In this same way—although harder to explain—I can do something with my words, with my voice, my body language, my tone, to persuade you to do something, to do this and not that, to do that and not this. I work at a very subliminal level in reading and directing other people. There's give and take—it's partly about the information I get from you through your body language, your words, your expressions, but it's also about the information that I put out there. My body language and expressions, my words, my tone of voice. This is the psychological side of persuasion. In some ways, humans are easily persuaded—just look at the scams we fall for. We are conned and misled by people all the time, by everyone from salespeople to psychopaths. In my case, I have the added advantage of the power and focus of my mind. When I combine the two, it's dangerous. People don't stand a chance. They will be persuaded to have a good time at my show!

How many nines are there between one and one hundred? Count them up: nine, nineteen, twenty-nine . . . all the way up to one hundred.

How many? Now turn the page for the answer.

The answer is twenty. Are you surprised? I know I persuaded you to see the problem in a certain way. But what about ninety, ninety-one, ninety-two, ninety-three, ninety-four, ninety-five, ninety-six, ninety-seven, and ninety-eight?

Isn't persuasion great?

Now I'll show you an image.

What did you see, an old woman or a young one? Does it matter that you saw one and not the other? Probably not. Could I have persuaded your brain to see one instead of the other? Absolutely.

Now un-jumble these sentences and read them.

    1.   animals some to carrots like eat
    2.   hear long better ears
    3.   quickly hopping fun is
    4.   live burrow rabbits in deep a

Take a look at this illusion. Which animal do you see?

You should have seen a rabbit, given that your brain had been primed to think about rabbits by unjumbling the sentences above. This particular case is not very subtle, but it's a good example of how you can be made to think about something or to want something by the power of suggestion. Influence. Persuasion. They are incredibly important skills for a mentalist.

The Psychology of Persuasion: Making Minds Think Alike—and Act Alike

Now you are probably wondering if I can teach you to persuade someone to pick a certain number between one and one hundred. Probably not. But I can show you some of the basic elements of persuasion that I use in my shows and my everyday life, and give you a greater understanding of them—and maybe persuade you to try them out yourself.

One of the most important elements of persuasion is creating an emotional connection with another person. If we create this rapport, then the other person is more likely to take notice of us, listen to us—and be persuaded by us.

When I'm performing in front of a live audience, whether it's at a big venue, a TV show, or at a private party, I want to get the audience to like me and to connect with me on an emotional level. As soon as they do, the show will go much better. They will open up to me more and become more persuadable. I can even make a mistake and they'll still think I'm cool.

I try to set up the emotional connection as soon as the audience sees me. You only have that one chance to make a first impression, so I go out of my way to impress upon the audience exactly what I want them to see. I always come out onto the stage running, with my arms stretched forward and open, with a wide, almost cartoon smile on my face. In this way, I get the audience to respond. They feel energized by my enthusiasm, they lean forward eagerly responding to the "hug" I've given them. And they smile. Smiling is contagious. Within moments of the welcoming applause dying down, I tell a joke.

"Before we start, I have to ask a question." Notice I say "we," not "I." I make us into friends, accomplices—we're all in this together—from the beginning. Then I single out someone in the audience, someone with a friendly, open face. "You! Over there! Say your name out loud." The friendly-faced guy responds, "John." "You are correct!" Everyone laughs. And if smiling is contagious, laughter is more so. The emotional connection is set up.

Now I'm going to try a bit of humor on you, just to build our personal connection and make you like me better. See if you can read these words. Don't worry if you can't at first, you'll probably need to step back, away from the book.

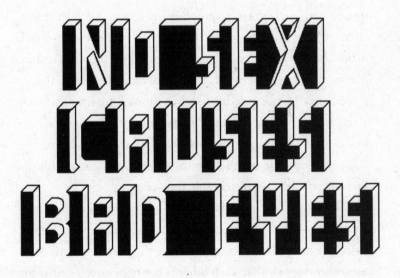

Now do you like me more?

Did you ever hear of something called mirroring? It's really cool. Picture yourself sitting in a bar waiting for a friend. You've ordered a drink, looked through the menu three times, updated your Facebook status on your phone, and still your friend hasn't arrived. Bored, you start to check out the people around you. Your eyes are drawn to the couple at the table opposite. They're nothing special to look at but there's something about them. It's the way they're leaning toward each other, arms stretched across the table so their fingertips are almost touching. When she laughs, he laughs, too, and when they laugh together they both throw their heads back slightly. She starts in on a story, her voice fast and excited, the words lost in the noise of the bar. Now he's speaking at the same rapid pace, now she cuts in, and their conversation gallops back and forth. They're so in tune with each other, so emotionally connected, you think. Then a funny thing happens. The woman suddenly leans back in her chair. Two seconds later, the guy does the same thing. Five seconds later, the woman leans forward. Followed almost immediately by the guy. It's like he's mimicking her. You look at the woman but she doesn't seem to mind, doesn't seem to notice. And the longer you look, you see that sometimes the woman follows the man's actions, sometimes the man follows the woman's. It's completely subconscious.

The couple in the bar is unconsciously mirroring each other's actions—their gestures, expressions, choice of words, even their breathing. They do this because they feel very safe with each other, very close to each other. They're in love. Their emotional connection runs deep. If this is the case—and this kind of mirroring happens with all kinds of people who know each other well—then the question becomes: if feeling connected to another person creates mirroring, will mirroring, in its turn, create a close connection between people? Richard Bandler, one of the developers of Neuro-linguistic Programming, set out to test this theory, and he proved that it can. By mirroring someone else's body movements or facial expressions, people can create a feeling of connection in that person. When I smile my great big smile on stage, I know that the audience members will smile back at me, and in turn I'll smile at them. This loop creates a connection. It's the same with laughter.

In a study at Duke University, psychologists Robin Tanner and Tanya Chartrand had thirty-seven students try out Vigor, a so-called new sports drink, and then answer a few questions about it. Nothing mind-blowing there. Except that about half of the students had their movements mirrored by the person interviewing them. If the student crossed his legs, a couple of seconds later the interviewer did the same. If the student touched her nose, played with her hair, leaned forward in her chair, then the interviewer would wait for a moment and then mimic the action.

None of the students noticed the mirroring, and all students— mirrored or not—were given identical interviews. And guess what? By the end of their interview, the mirrored students were much more likely than the non-mirrored ones to say they would buy the drink Vigor and to think it would be a successful product. And the mirrored students were even more positive about the drink if they knew that the interviewer had a personal stake in the product's success. Interesting, right? The mirroring had created an emotional connection. But the important part is that no one noticed. It's a very subtle process.

So why does mirroring work? It's pretty simple really. We feel comfortable with people who are like us in many ways—maybe we're the same age, from the same country or state, or we're both crazy about the same baseball team—or we both despise the same team. We like people who get us. It makes sense, then, that we feel at ease with someone who has similar body language to us or uses the same kind of verbal expressions—even if it's at a subconscious level.

Think of emotional connection as a way of communicating better with people, and mirroring as one of the ways to attain this. Subtlety is key, though! If you're in a job interview or on a date, it's probably not a good idea to start mimicking every gesture a second after the other person performs it. The idea is to be a slow, slightly imperfect mirror. If you follow actions too closely, then other people will notice. And that will be the end of any feelings of goodwill—then it's just creepy, and you can kiss the job or a second date good-bye.

If the other person scratches their nose, there's no need for violently rubbing your own. Instead just adopt a similar posture to the person you're with. Are they sitting or standing, leaning to the left or right? You could do that, too. Is their head forward? Where are their hands? Are their arms crossed? Be open to the tone of voice, their facial expression, and subtly copy that—laugh when they do, but do it naturally. Listen to words that they use and use those words, too. Do they use the word "cool" or "amazing"? Then you can, too, and the connection will increase. People respond better when they're spoken to in their own "language." Notice things like the speed, volume, and pitch of their speech—and match your speech to it. The other person will relax and conversation will flow more smoothly. Eventually the rapport will be so great that the mirroring will just happen naturally.

Emotional connection with an audience is much harder than with one other person, and it is hugely important for my particular kind of entertainment. It's a strong element of my show and increases my power to persuade, my power to read minds, and my power to draw upon my chi energy. Whenever I'm communicating with the audience, there's a kind of game going on, a dance. I'm sending out subliminal directives to control their responses, but I'm also reading their nonverbal clues. Of course, I'm reading specific minds, too. There's a huge amount of information being communicated back and forth. When I interact with one audience member, it's as if I'm creating a map of that person's mind based on everything I can read about them, both inside and outside their mind, and it seems to spread out around them as they interact with other members of the audience, and with me. It's like a web.

One of my favorite acts of persuasion is one that gets those webs of emotional connection tangling throughout the entire audience. It's really cool. It goes like this.

Paris, 2008
400 PEOPLE

"I need someone I can trust," I say, waving a large, brown envelope in the air. "To keep this safe." I'm in the middle of the audience in the middle of my act. "You," I say, pointing over several rows to a woman with a nice smile. "Will you keep this safe for me?" She nods and laughs, looking a bit embarrassed. I pass the envelope to her.

"What's your name?"

"Lindsey."

"Okay, Lindsey, so this envelope has something in it that I wrote earlier, and your job is to keep the envelope safe." I hold up the envelope so that everyone in the audience can see that it has about a million staples around it and whatever is in there is not going to come out easily, or secretly.

I pass it back to Lindsey, then approach a man in the row behind her and say, "So. Could you tell me the name of a woman that there is no chance that I know." The man thinks for a moment. "But be careful," I add. "I know lots of women." Everyone laughs.

The man grins and says, "Emma." I write the name EMMA on a big whiteboard so that everyone in the audience can see. Now I move through the audience and choose someone else. "Could you tell me the name of a country that you've never visited?" The country GERMANY gets written on the board, and I move the microphone along to another person, in a different section of the audience. That person has to name a celebrity they like. Now we have GEORGE CLOONEY written up on the board. Everyone in the audience is leaning forward. They're excited. They're not sure what to expect. They're all working together as an audience to create a narrative. "I knew you were going to say George," I say. "I have a picture of him in my pocket." Everyone is astonished. I hear different voices nearby. "No! You have his picture? Wow!" I hold up a photo of a bald baby. "This is George when he was two years old." Everyone laughs. We move on.

Another person has the microphone now. "Which kind of car would you choose?"

"A Buick."

"A Buick?? Are you sure? Not a Porsche? Why would he choose a Buick and not a Porsche?" I ask the audience. They all laugh. A BUICK is added to the list. The next person has to imagine how much they would win at a casino. $10,010. Very tricky of them. Then the microphone is passed one more time. I say to the next person, "Imagine you're going on vacation. How long are you going for?" I add his response to the whiteboard. Now we have a list of EMMA, GERMANY, GEORGE CLOONEY, BUICK, $10,010, TEN DAYS. Everyone looks at me with anticipation. The whole audience is involved, because I have asked them to join together to come up with a narrative. They're part of the act and they're vested in it.

Now I look over at Lindsey. "You still have the envelope?" I ask. She nods, laughing, holding the envelope up for all to see. "Well, could you come over here then and open it?" She makes her way through the audience to me, where I'm standing with the microphone and whiteboard. She tugs open the envelope, all around the staples, and pulls out a piece of paper. She looks at me expectantly. "Go ahead," I say. "Read it."

She starts to read. It's a letter. "Hi, everyone. I am so happy to write you this letter. I am still traveling and I'm in Germany now. Yesterday I was at a big party and it was fun. You're not going to believe me but I met George Clooney." She stops reading. People in the audience are looking at each other, murmuring. They're starting to be amazed. "He was so nice he even gave me a ride in his old Buick."

The excitement in the audience is crazy now. It's contagious. I have to hold up my hand to calm people down. "I've been having a great time, especially at the casino where I won $10,000 at blackjack."

"Only $10,000?" I say, pointing to the whiteboard that says $10,010. I shrug. It's not too bad.

"It's very close," says Lindsey kindly, and then continues to read. "I also won $10 on the slot machines." Now everyone is laughing, surprised. "There's no way! There's no way!" shouts a voice nearby. Lindsey has to wait a while before continuing. "I should be home in eight days." There's a whisper of disappointment in the audience that it doesn't say ten days. I say, "Never mind, it's okay, let's move on."

Lindsey reads again, "But I've been told the flight will have a two-day delay." At this, everyone roars with laughter and shouts out, delighted. "Say hi to everyone and especially to Lindsey who's reading this right now. Signed, Emma." Lindsey is standing with the microphone in utter shock, her mouth hanging open. People in the audience leap to their feet, applauding and laughing. They're all amazed. They can't believe what just happened. I can see people saying, "How did he do that?" And they go through the whole process in their minds again. It's open prediction at work on a large scale. Persuasion. It's crazy.

Body Language: Let's Get Physical

I love the letter-reading segment of the show, because it involves so many different people from the audience. It also makes me hyperaware of another important aspect of my work as a mentalist. The importance of body language. I use it as a tool for persuading and reading my audience all the time. During my performances, I often call on people from the audience to help me. I never just pick random people. I pick people who I think will work best for a certain segment of the show. It's all part of the process of being able to influence someone.

What do I mean by this? As I've said, when I do a show my connection with the audience is hugely important. Very often I'll go out into the theater lobby before a show and study people in the lines where they're buying tickets or waiting. I'll watch them closely and think about my victims . . . sorry, volunteers . . . for the experiments in the show. I like to get a sense of my audience, read their body language, their emotions, and work out what kind of a reaction they might have to my show. Some people are nervous when they meet me. They're guarded and shut down as if they're scared I can read every thought in their mind. That's one of the main reasons I use humor during my performances.

Pretty early in my career, I discovered that my mental skills can make some people uncomfortable. They're unsure what to expect and feel vulnerable and at a disadvantage around me. So I tell jokes. I laugh. I put people at ease. Most people warm up to me after a quick introduction, but others stay closed and unsure. They don't want me to read their mind. I'm not going to pick someone like that during my act—it's hard to read the mind of someone who really doesn't want it read. Sometimes I'll watch the audience unseen as they file into the auditorium. Again, I'll read their movements. Are they excited, nervous, bored, skeptical?

Even as the show is in progress, I'll be scanning the audience for people's reactions, thinking they might be good for a certain part of the show. Sometimes I'll speak to an audience member—"How are you tonight?"—just so I can see the reaction of the person sitting next to them. It's amazing what information is given out through our body language—and I'm processing it all the time.

Researchers have shown that when watching a body's movements reduced to points of light on a screen, observers can still read grief, anger, joy, disgust, fear, and surprise. A research team led by Dr. Winand Dittrich at the University of Hertfordshire, England, worked with trained dancers to investigate just how easy it is to interpret emotion by reading body language only. Research participants watched short video clips of two dancers, one male, one female, and attempted to work out the emotions conveyed by the dancers' movements. Some participants watched fully lit scenes of the dancer, while others watched while the dancer moved in the dark with thirteen points of light clipped to the body. For the fully lit scenes, 88 percent of participants were correct in guessing the emotions portrayed, while for the points-of-light scenes, 63 percent were correct—way above chance. A few years later, the experiment was repeated using only six light points attached to a dancer's shoulders, wrists, and ankles. Amazingly, participants were still 62 percent accurate in their interpretations of emotions. We're primed to read emotion and meaning into body movement—even when there's very little to go on.

One of the staples of my show—and especially when I'm invited onto talk shows—is when I'll guess the name of someone's first love. I do this partly by reading the mind directly and partly by reading the body. I'll ask specific questions that draw a verbal reaction but also that set off a chain of facial expressions that can give me clues. If I ask how many letters the name has, I can literally see the person counting the letters by watching their face. Some people even count on their fingers without realizing it. So I narrow down my options in this way and let that guide the actual mind-reading.

We've all heard about eye movements and the way people look in a certain direction when they're lying. It's true. The eyes are windows not just into the soul but the mind, too. Most of us, when we're talking to someone, focus on their eyes. It's the easiest place to look on someone's face. But we don't look in a way that actually lets us see. We don't really think about it. We're operating on autopilot again. The next time you're talking to someone, try and watch the way their eyes move, just for fun, just to see how those movements fit into the conversation. You might be amazed.

Here's something very interesting that I want you to learn. Not many people know about Visual Accessing Cues. They are discussed by Richard Bandler and John Grinder in their book *Frogs into Princes: Neuro Linguistic Programming.*" From their experiments, this is what they found.

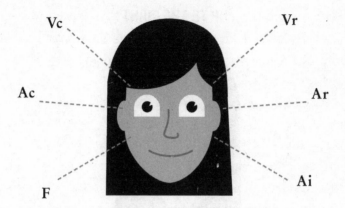

Ask someone a question and see which way they look. These directions are for a right-handed person and are from your viewpoint. So, if they look:

UP TO THE LEFT

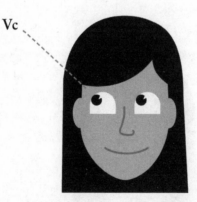

This is for **"Visually Constructed Images"** (Vc). When you ask someone to imagine something, their eyes move up to the left so they can "visually construct" in their mind. Imagine a three-legged giraffe—eyes move up to the left.

UP TO THE RIGHT

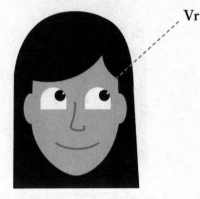

Vr

This is for **"Visually Remembered Images"** (Vr). When you ask someone to tell you about an experience they've had, their eyes move up to the right while they "visually remember." What did you eat for lunch? Eyes up to the right. Think about it. Chicken noodle soup.

TO THE LEFT

Ac

This is for **"Auditory Constructed"** (Ac). When you ask someone to make up a tune, their eyes move to the left as they do a little "auditory construction" in their mind. Create a new symphony—eyes to the left.

TO THE RIGHT

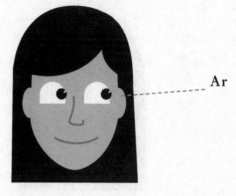

Ar

This is for **"Auditory Remembered"** (Ar). When you ask someone to sing a song they know, their eyes will move to the right as they "auditorily remember." Sing a Lady Gaga song—eyes to the right. "Poker Face."

DOWN TO THE LEFT

F

This is for **Feeling** (F). When you ask someone to recall a smell, taste, or feeling, their eyes go down to the left. What did the chicken soup you had for lunch taste like? Eyes down to the left.

DOWN TO THE RIGHT

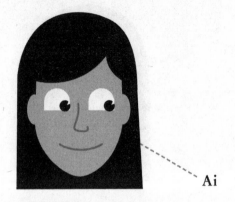

Ai

This is for **Internal Dialog (Auditory Internal)** (Ai). When someone is talking to themselves, their eyes will be down to the right.

On a basic level, when you ask someone a question, if they're telling the truth their eyes should go up to the right (as you are facing them) as they remember something that happened. Up to the left would mean a "constructed" or imagined image—a lie. It can be really interesting just to watch people's eye movements, because usually we don't pay any attention to them at all. The more you watch, the more you can read. But remember, this is not mathematically precise, so don't take it too literally. These clues are subtle and should be taken into account with other information. Don't think that if your wife looks in a certain direction she's cheating on you. This is just one ingredient in a whole recipe.

When taken into account with other elements of body language, this is all vital information for me as a mentalist. It's another way of connecting with another person's mind.

Johannesburg, 2010
1,500 People

I've invited a man up onto the stage and given him a $100 bill. It's a nice-size bill. I've asked him to hide it in one hand and, if I don't guess the hand correctly, he gets to keep the money. Of course I guess correctly. Simple body-language reading. It's not such a big deal. Then I invite up two more people and get them to hide the bill. So there are four hands. It's still easy. Next I ask ten or fifteen more people up onto the stage and I tell them, "Here's $100. Take fifteen seconds and choose just one of you to hold the bill." Music plays and the lights zoom in as they all go off to the other side of the stage and discuss who'll hold the money. After fifteen seconds or so they come back and I ask them all to stand in a row with their two hands out in front of them, fists tightly clenched. At this point, I tell them if I don't guess who's holding the bill then each of them will win $100. It becomes a challenge game. This creates a buzz on stage and in the audience, and I see everyone on stage take the game a little more seriously, shifting their positions and poses.

It's a nice moment in the show, with lights and music and this group of people standing there with their hands out, in anticipation. I'm happy to see the people who don't have the money trying so hard to look like they do, like they're trying to hide something, and the person with the money trying to look so cool, as if he hasn't a care in the world. They're all playing with body language.

So then I use my skills to figure everything out. People often ask me how much I use my skills and how much of it is psychology. It changes every time. It depends on the people on stage, the people in the audience, even which country I'm in. The psychology part includes reading people's body language—their body position, facial expression, and their eye movements. Sometimes I explain people's body language to the audience and that makes everything funnier. Like now. There's one guy who's holding the money in his hand straight out in front of him. I slip behind him and say, "So how do you feel?" He says, "Fine," but he's turning his whole body away from me. I turn to the audience. "You see, he's shielding his hand."

So much of body language is remembering to read it. The clues are right there in front of us. Everyone in the audience starts laughing, because they look and see that it's true. The guy is stretching his arm away from me, behind his body. Then I say, "That's the hand with the money." He shakes his head, but everything else about his body language is screaming to me that he has the money. And, sure enough, the guy opens up his hand and there's the folded $100 bill. Reading body language has saved me a lot of money over time! To be honest, during my entire professional career I've lost about $500. But even then, it was funny, so I was okay with it.

The method I use for that routine is 90-percent based on reading people's eyes, the same method I just taught you, which you can use whenever you want.

> **IT'S REALLY FUN TO WATCH THIS PERFORMANCE. SEE IT FOR YOURSELF AT WWW.MINDREADERBOOK.COM/MONEY**

Putting Words to Work

Speaking is something we do every day, all the time, and we really don't think about it. We move through most conversations on autopilot, words just falling out of our mouths. Instead, we need to understand the power of language, of certain words, and actively think about what we say. We can use the power of our minds—and our knowledge of other people's minds—to be as persuasive as possible when we speak.

The French eighteenth-century writer and philosopher Voltaire was right when he said, "Give me ten minutes to talk away my ugly face and I will bed the Queen of France." He knew that words can be incredibly powerful and persuasive in getting what—or whom—you want, much more so than just having a handsome face. There's a book I love, about the art of seduction, *The Game* by Neil Strauss—there, too, you'll find the importance of words and the amazing effects they can have on other people when used in just the right way.

So I'd like to teach you some secret tips about the language of persuasion.

Some words create strong basic impressions in our minds when we hear them. You remember that rhyme from when you were a kid, "Sticks and stones may break your bones, but words can never hurt you?" Don't believe it. Words can hit us with a lot of force. They can hurt and harm, but they can also be positive—and very persuasive. Mark Twain once said the difference between the right word and the almost right word is "the difference between lightning and a lightning bug."

The first powerful word to know is "because." This word holds a huge emotional sway over us. Think back to your childhood, when your parents asked you to do something (or not to do something). "Lior, don't take the TV apart again." "But, Dad, I just wanted to see—" "Lior, I said no." "But why, Dad?" And then we get the response that all of us are so familiar with: "Because I said so." Or, "Just because." That word is shorthand for so many possibilities. When we were kids, it meant that we could question no further, limits had been pushed far enough, that parental authority had spoken, that further discussion would result in punishment. And now, when we hear the word "because," it still acts powerfully upon us.

On a practical level, if you make a request and include the word "because" in the sentence, your request is more likely to be fulfilled because of the power of that one word. What's really fascinating is that many people will not even listen to the reason following your "because," no matter how crazy it is.

Robert Cialdini, author of one of my favorite books, *Influence, the Psychology of Persuasion,* writes: "A well-known principle of human behavior says that when we ask someone to do us a favor we will be more successful if we provide a reason. People simply like to have reasons for what they do." And what better way to introduce a reason than the word "because"?

Cialdini cites this great example. Ellen Langer, professor of psychology at Harvard University, conducted a research study around a library photocopying machine. A researcher showed up and asked to cut in line. "Excuse me, could I cut in line?" As expected, most people said no. Why should they let that person go ahead of them? Make them wait like everyone else. However, when that same person asked to cut in line and gave a reasonable excuse—"because I have just one page to copy," or "because I'm running late for an appointment"—a lot of people agreed. That's interesting in itself. What's crazy is that even when the reason given for cutting in line was completely irrational ("because I have copies to make," or maybe "because it's raining," or "because I'm hungry"), more people agreed than when the word "because" was not used and so no reason was given. The word creates a sense of logic, or makes people regress into childhood memories, and allows us to be persuaded.

If you happen to have a persuasive speech to write, then use the word "because" a lot. It joins ideas together in a nice flow that listeners like, because thoughts get tied together, slide into a listener's subconscious, and don't meet with much resistance. We expect the word "because" to make everything logical, so most of the time we don't take the time to figure out if what's being said is really true. Mentalists are very persuasive because they wear bright colors. Really? And remember all those advertisers who use the expression "Because you deserve it"? We can't argue with that. Did you know that most of those commercials are aimed at women? The advertisers really know what they're doing.

The second important word is "now." Again, this takes us back to our childhoods, to that moment when parental requests turned impatient and we knew that it was time to act—or else. "Lior, stop bothering your brothers with your mind games NOW!" That would get the desired response quickly—and my brothers would breathe a sigh of relief. The word "now" suggests a sense of urgency and adds a wakeup call to the listener, that not only do you expect this request to be met and carried out, but that you expect it to be carried out immediately. NOW. That made you jump. Think about all the TV infomercials that you've seen that use the words "call now," or "pick up the phone now." These are direct calls to action—and they work.

When you come to one of my shows, you might try and listen to see how often I use these words. Do I use the word "now" when I'm asking someone which word they want to choose in a book? Or the word "because" when I'm asking someone to think of a number between one and one hundred? It doesn't really work like that. I'm working on so many different levels of persuasion, in subliminal ways. I use these words all the time in my off-stage life with my managers, my girl-friend, celebrities, and potential clients. I like to say that any time I have a face-to-face meeting, I get the deal closed. And so can you.

The third and fourth words on the list of important and powerful words go together. "Please" and "thank you." And yes, they take us right back to childhood, too. We all remember our parents with their helpful hints of "Now, what do we say?" We automatically knew to fill in the blanks with the correct response of "please" or "thank you." Or, remember the phrase, "What's the magic word"? "Please" has always been the magic word and it still opens doorways. Psychologically, "please" softens commands and gives the impression that the person being asked to do something has a degree of control. When we say "please" to someone, it makes that person feel good, and in return they like us more, and because they like us more they are more willing to do something for us. When we say "thank you," again we make the other person feel positive toward us, and they're more likely to help us another time, because they see that their actions are appreciated. In my shows, I always make a point to thank people who come up on stage and help me in my act, and I get the audience to give them a big round of applause, too. I'm genuinely appreciative, but I also know that it helps with the positive emotional connections that are at work.

In social psychology, the phrase "thank you" puts us in the realm of something called the law of reciprocity. I'd like you to really remember to use this tip, as it's an incredibly powerful persuasion tool, and all it involves is the well-timed placing of a few seemingly innocent words. As humans, we are conditioned to follow the laws of reciprocity. When someone buys you a gift or invites you over for dinner, you feel duty-bound to follow up with a gift or a dinner invitation. It's just part of the way we operate socially. It happens with individuals, groups, even governments. A newspaper story about reciprocity made a very strong impression on me. In 1999, there was a terrible earthquake in Turkey, and Israel sent over some assistance despite strained relations between the two countries. Last year—when relations were even worse—Turkey sent Israel two fire-fighting aircraft to help contain a devastating brush fire, because it felt indebted to Israel by the law of reciprocity.

So how can you use this rule to your advantage? The next time you do a favor for someone, think carefully about what you say when they thank you for your help. Do not say, "No problem" or "It was my pleasure." Instead, invoke reciprocity. Say, "I know you would do the same for me." Now you have secretly implanted a message of indebtedness in their brain—and get ready to cash in at the favor bank the next time you need to persuade them to do something for you.

Here's another word that I find gets great results in persuading people: "imagine." John Lennon obviously knew what he was doing. The clever thing about the word "imagine" is that you invite the person you're trying to persuade to visualize your suggestion in their own mind. In this way, it becomes very real to them. It moves from being your request to something that they've thought of. In time, their subconscious may even think that they created the thought themselves. Not only have you persuaded someone to consider your request, you've also managed to make it seem like you didn't even make the request! This is genius at work. It's also the premise for the amazing movie *Inception,* except that they plant the thought into the layers of a dream. As part of my show, I'll use the word "imagine" to get people to think of the name of a movie star, or a country they've never visited. Sometimes I'll add, "And if you don't have a good imagination, just imagine that you have one."

Advertisers use the power of "imagine" all the time. "Imagine yourself on the white sands of Florida." "Imagine yourself behind the wheel of a BMW." Before you know it, you'll have forgotten how or when the word and image were implanted in your mind. All you'll know would be that you have a strong desire to visit Florida or buy a certain luxury car. They have now become your own private wishes.

Very often, when you're working on persuading someone, you're trying to get them to respond with that other magic word: "yes." "Yes, Lior, we'd like you to appear on our morning talk show." "Yes, Lior, I did say the words 'million-dollar contract.'" Let's face it—the word "yes" has a nice ring to it and we all like to hear it in connection with our life goals and dreams. And the date for Saturday night we've been trying to set up.

But what about that other word, the deadly nemesis of "yes"? The dreaded "no" that we don't want to hear in response to our request. Is there anything we can do about the word "no"? Yes! Yes, there is. Imagine that you've gone to your boss to ask for a pay raise. You've done everything you can to be persuasive but somehow your boss has remained immune to your powers and your charm, and she's said the one word you don't want to hear. "No." There it is.

Now, the worst thing you can do at this point is to say, "Oh well, thanks for listening anyway," head glumly back to your desk, and have a generally bad day. Your boss is human. And nearly all humans like to please their fellow humans, because that's the way we're wired. Saying no actually makes people feel bad. Now that your boss has said no is when she is most vulnerable to saying yes, to make the situation better. Now is your time to strike. Either you can ask for a smaller pay raise, or you could ask for something unrelated to the pay raise but that would mean a lot to you. Maybe some extra vacation time, or attendance at a conference you've always wanted to go to. Your boss is much more likely to say yes to this request at this point than if you wait and ask her a week later.

When you try this persuasive technique, you're employing the very effective psychological principle of relative value. Salespeople know to offer a product—a suit or a bottle of wine—at a higher price so that a lower-priced product (but probably more expensive than you were hoping) will seem like a bargain in comparison. Just as warm water seems cold after you've placed your hand in hot water.

Let's think about the example of wine for a moment. Imagine that the wine sommelier recommends three wines from the extensive wine menu. She offers you a wine at $35, one at $55, and one at $80. It's a birthday celebration, and you're willing to splurge. Which one do you choose? Probably the one at $55. You don't want to seem cheap, but $80 seems like a lot of money. Now what if the sommelier had offered you wines at $115, $80, $55, and $35? It's highly likely that you would consider the $80 wine—now it doesn't seem so expensive, right? Just as your boss will consider your request reasonable when it's sandwiched next to a higher request.

Here's a little mind game to illustrate this point. Look at the two interior circles. Which do you think is bigger?

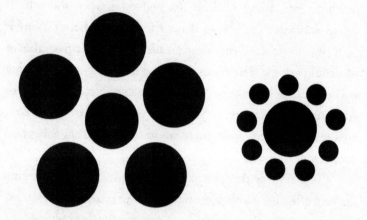

Probably you said the one on the right? It does look bigger. But, surprisingly enough, they're the exact same size! It all has to do with the size of the circles surrounding them. Again, it's all about the concept of relative value, or, in this case, relative size.

Remember to make it work for you as a negotiating tool.

Another persuasive language tool I use all the time is this: never give the person you're speaking with the opportunity to say no—unless you want them to. Instead of saying, "Would you like to see a movie?" which could result in a negative, I'll say something like "Which day is good for a movie, Wednesday or Thursday?" Then things move forward. A date! Or, after meeting a potential business contact, I'll say, "Is it best to call or e-mail you?" They're not going to respond "Neither," or "Whatever you do, Lior, please don't," so when they say, "Oh, e-mail's probably better because I travel a lot," I've received an invitation from them to e-mail. And I'm always polite and follow up every time.

You can also try the yes-ladder technique from Neil Strauss's book *The Game*. First you ask a series of questions that elicit a yes response. Next you ask a question where you really want a positive response, and you'll often get one, as a pattern has already been established.

But of all the words, which do you think has the strongest emotional attachments for us? No, it's not "money." It's our name. It's a word that goes all the way back, in most cases, to the moment of our birth when our parents first whisper it to us. Over the years our names have been said to us in so many different ways: in anger, love, disappointment, resentment, drunkenness, hilarity. You name it, it's been said in that way. Even though most of us share our names with many other people, it still resonates. In crowds, we hear our name called above the rest even when we're not being addressed. Our names spark a reaction from us.

Whenever I speak with someone during my shows or invite them up onto the stage, I ask for their name. It creates that emotional connection I'm aiming for. If you are introduced to someone new, say their name back to them. "I'd like you to meet my friend Lior, the amazing mentalist." "Hello, Lior, it's nice to meet you." Immediately Lior (the amazing mentalist) is impressed, consciously or subconsciously—it doesn't matter which. You've made a connection, a bond between you, just by that one mention of his name.

Now that you're feeling all pleased with yourself, this is the exact moment you're about to blow the progress you've made. Because now you probably think it would be a good idea to say the name lots of times, to spread it throughout the conversation, just to prove that you remember it and that you're such a great new friend. Big mistake. Each time you say the name now, your rating in Lior's eyes will drop, and continue to drop, and you'll seem like a phony salesperson. But if you say the name once at the beginning of the conversation and—wait for it—once again as you're leaving the conversation, then your ranking will rocket up in Lior's estimation. And you might receive a call from the amazing mentalist in the morning.

Whenever I'm doing my "think of a number" act, I always ask the person their name first. Then I'll write their name down on my little card or the whiteboard along with the number. Like this. "John will say 31." Again, it sets up a connection right away. Now the person feels special, because I've done this performance especially for them. It's their name, their number, their moment.

As you can see, the words we use and the ways in which we use them are important. And when you're speaking with someone, remember to use eye contact. In an average conversation, the two people talking with each other do not look at each other in equal amounts. The listener looks directly at the talker around 75 percent of the time. The talker looks at the listener only about 40 percent of the time. If you want to persuade the person you're talking to, then look at them more. It's as simple as that. Try to get the figure up to 50 percent. Anything more than that, it starts to seem weird and your listener will wonder why you're staring at them so much and will stop listening to your fantastic flow of persuasive words. It makes sense. People like to be addressed. They like to be shown attention and respect. Did you know that some troops in Iraq were forbidden from wearing sunglasses when speaking to Iraqis, specifically so they could make eye contact with local citizens, a sign of respect?

I'm very big on eye contact. I'll often peer into people's eyes when I'm reading their minds. You can read so much about someone through the eyes. During a normal conversation, I'll make sure to make eye contact. My humor and playful touch show up in my eyes and when that is conveyed other people feel more comfortable in my presence. They relax—and become open to my influence. And here's a very special secret tip that I'd like to share with you. I have a very powerful look that I've created and developed over time—a strong stare—for important moments. Instead of staring into someone's eyes, stare at the bridge of their nose. It still looks like you're staring into the other person's eyes but it means that your eyes won't flicker around and you'll be able to hold their gaze for a long time. This creates a deep, serious look that is extremely impressive and persuasive. I use it as a power look and it really gets results. Try it on your friends and family. How do they feel under your new authoritative gaze?

Standing in front of an audience, I feel like a puppet master, holding all the strings of communication and persuasion that have been generated during a performance. I like the image. I can see it clearly, the webs of thoughts and the power of those thoughts crisscrossing throughout the audience. But, despite my best efforts, I'm not always in control. A simple line of communication can be down.

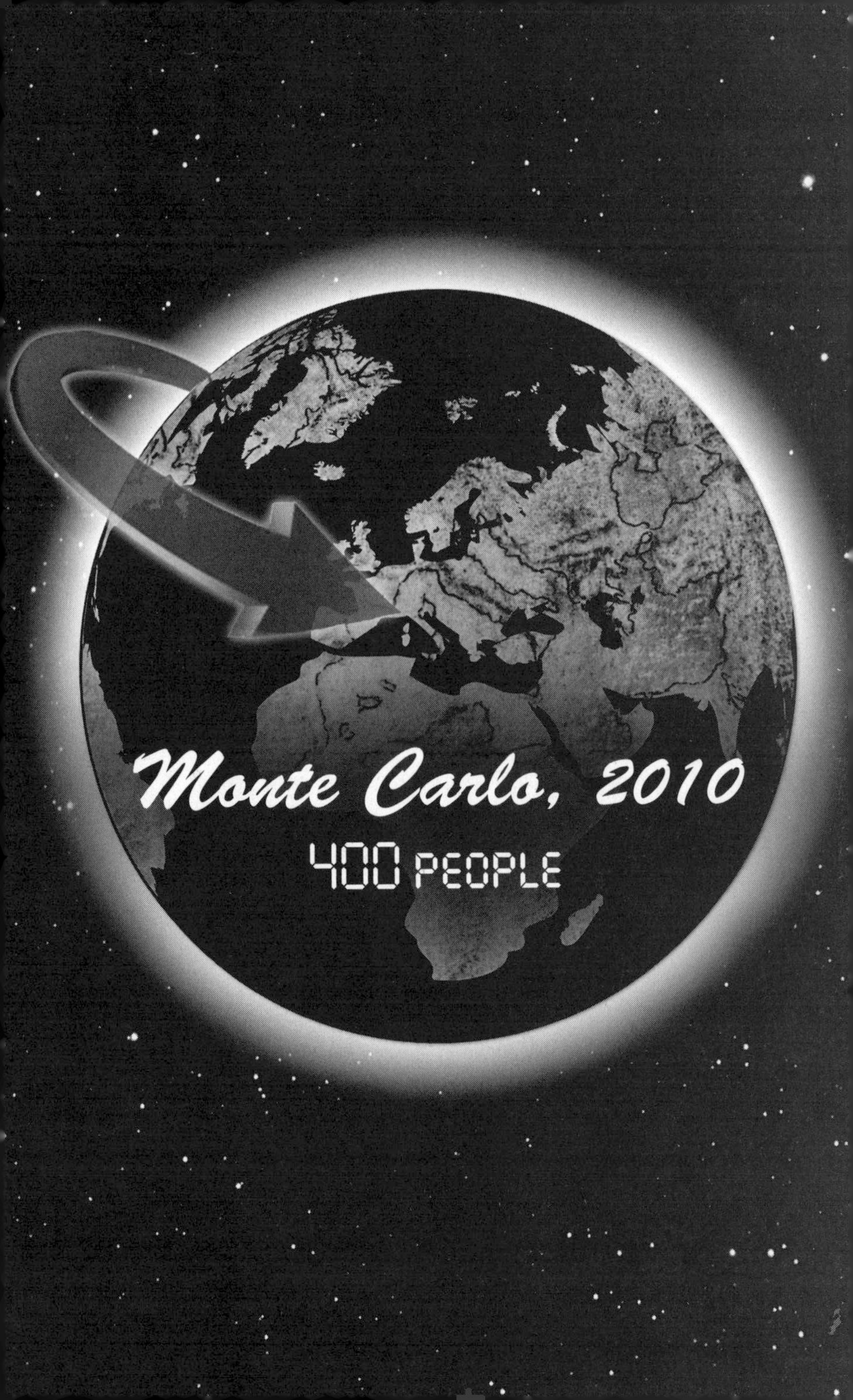
Monte Carlo, 2010
400 PEOPLE

I'm up on stage and I call someone up to help me with my next portion of the show. I give the man a closed envelope and 10 euro and tell him to go and play the roulette table, then to come back and tell us how he did. He seems very excited by the idea as he runs off stage and over to the casino next door. I had picked him specifically for this act. I banter with the audience and we wait with much anticipation for the man to return. The music plays and the lights strobe across the stage and through the audience. Will he have won or lost?

After a few minutes, the man rushes back into the room and back up on stage. He looks out of breath. The audience cheers. "So, my friend," I ask him. "What happened?"

"Nothing," he says and he shrugs. He is giving off strange, defensive body language.

"What do you mean, nothing?" I'm really surprised by his response.

"Well, the minimum bet for the roulette table is 20 euro. And you only gave me 10 euro." He hands me the money and the envelope. At this, the audience roars with laughter. I'm laughing, too, while the guy just looks embarrassed.

"You realize you just ruined this part of the show," I say. The guy smiles and looks sheepish. The audience is loving it. "You didn't think of adding your own 10 euro to my 10 euro?" I add. At this, the guy heads off the stage while I say to the still-laughing audience, "So if you ever want to see this part of my show, you'll have to come back another night."

Luckily, this takes place toward the end of the show. All my emotional connections have been set up and the audience is fol-lowing my lead, laughing when I want them to laugh, focusing when

I want them to focus, and so they are able to follow my lead here, too. I go with the flow and laugh even though things haven't gone according to plan. It helps to have the audience on your side.

So, did I make a mistake in choosing that guy to help me out? Sometimes I wonder about that. Did I not read his body language properly? Did I fail to persuade him to do what I wanted? I don't think so. He seemed willing and open enough. But something unforeseen happened when he was out of the room. Persuasion and body language can only go so far. The best I could do in this situation was to laugh and move on—but to remember and learn for the next time. Limit the opportunities for my helpers to act without my influence. And make sure I know the minimum bet for the roulette table at any place I'm performing. Now I call this story "The Guy Who Didn't Gamble," and it has become part of my show's banter. He could have won!

What would have happened if a member of the audience had come back to my show the next evening? This is how the act would have gone. Lights, music, action. I invite someone up onto the stage and I ask a few questions. "How do you like Monte Carlo? Have you won any money yet? How would you like to win something tonight?" My helper nods his head vigorously at that. Next, I hand over 20 euro—no mistakes this time—and a sealed envelope and I ask him to go to the roulette table and place a bet. He disappears eagerly. Again, the audience and I wait. They're a receptive audience and I've built a really great rapport with them. When the man comes back, he runs up onto the stage and takes a bow; I think he has a bit of the stage gene in him, too. People in the audience lean forward in their seats. "So," I ask, "did you win the money?" The man shakes his head.

"Why not?" I ask. "Tell me what happened." The man looks like a naughty schoolboy now, as if he is in trouble. "I put the money on number twelve," he says. "And it wasn't the winning number, was it?" I ask. "No," he admits. "Number eight was the winning number." "Number eight," I say. "Oh well. Better luck next time." He looks at me as if I'm going to hand him another 20 euro. "With your own money," I say, and the audience laughs.

There's a pause then, while everyone wonders what's going to happen next. Thoughts start to run through everyone's mind. Did something go wrong, was the guy supposed to win? That's when I speak again. "By the way, did you happen to open the envelope?" The guy looks down at the envelope in his hand as if he's forgotten that it's there and shakes his head. "You didn't tell me to," he says defensively. "Why didn't you open the enve-lope?" "Because you didn't tell me to." The guy is almost yelling now. "So would you mind opening it now?" Which he does. He pulls out a folded piece of paper and looks back to me for guid-ance. "Could you please unfold the paper and read what is writ-ten there?" So the guy does this. He reads simply, "Please put the money on number eight." The guy's jaw drops and the crowd goes wild. It's a very strong scene.

The emotional connection between the audience and me at a moment like this is huge. It's electric. It's as if we're operating together, bound together by the power of persuasion. It's amaz-ing. And the other thing to consider is why didn't the man open the envelope? Had I created such a rapport between us that he didn't even think about it? I hadn't told him to do so, and so he didn't. He was completely under the power of my persuasion. Now, how did I do it? I'd have to kill you.

Las Vegas, 2011

900 People

We're back at my big show. I've guessed a number, guessed a name, and had Jane choose a number in a phone book that amazingly matched the number created randomly by the women in the front row. The women are still freaked out by this. I have Blake in charge of the money and a scroll.

And now I close my eyes for an instant, to still my mind. When I reopen them, I look out into the sea of faces, many of them familiar by now. They have connected as an audience, reacting like one being. Laughter. Shock. Amazement. At this moment, they're showing anticipation. I step to the middle of the stage.

"I need a couple from the audience. A man and a woman to help me with something amazing!" This time, a whole host of hands flies up into the air. I look over the volunteers. Whom to choose, whom to choose? I pick a couple way in the back of the room. They're laughing together, in tune with each other. They thread their way along their row and up to the stage, the man looking out for his wife, gently holding her elbow up the steps to the stage.

"Tell me, what are your names?"

"Pam."

"Steve." I move them slightly on the stage so they are standing a little way apart from each other, facing the audience, with me in the middle.

"Okay, I want you both to look straight ahead, close your eyes, and concentrate, because in a few seconds you're going to feel some weird sensations." I touch their shoulders.

"Each of us has something called chi. Our energy. Let me show you all what happens when I combine their energy together. Pam, in a few seconds, I'm going to touch you on the face." I touch Steve lightly on his nose. "Did you feel that, Pam?"

She nods, her eyes tightly closed. "Can you show me where I touched you?" Straight away, she points to her nose. No hesitation. I hear murmurs from the audience. "Okay, Pam, now you're going to feel a weird tickling." I touch Steve's chin and gently tickle it. "You feel it, right?"

Pam says, "Yes."

I look out into the audience with a grin. "Can you show me where?" Her hand flies straight to her chin.

Next I tweak Steve's back, not too hard, but hard enough that he twists away from me a little. Suddenly, Pam says, "Ouch." "Now, don't open your eyes and tell me if you felt something strange," I say to her.

"Yes." Pam is nodding.

"Really? What did you feel?"

"A pinch." There are exclamations of surprise from the audience. They're loving it. "A pinch? Where?" I don't really have to ask this last question. Pam is already pointing to her lower back, rubbing it as if it's slightly sore. "Amazing!" I say. "Now open your eyes." Pam blinks a little at the surroundings, and looks first at Steve, then at me. "How do you feel?" I ask her. She smiles.

"Good," she says slowly, waiting. She's trying to figure out what's up. "Let me tell you something," I add, my hand on her shoulder. "The audience is not applauding, because they are in shock." I nod out at the audience, laughing.

"Remember that I touched your nose?"

Pam says, "Yes." I turn to the audience.

"Did I touch her nose?"

Everyone shouts, "NO!" They are gleeful. Pam is bewildered.

"I didn't touch your nose. I was touching Steve's nose. Remember that I tickled you on the chin? Did I tickle her?"

"NO!" screams the audience, including Steve. He's laughing, caught up in everything.

"I didn't tickle you. I was tickling him. I didn't pinch your back, I was pinching his back!" Pam stands there, amazed, looking to Steve for confirmation. He's nodding and laughing, and reaches over to give Pam a hug. She's still shaking her head, unable to believe it.

"I felt it," she says to Steve, to me.

"So, do you know what this means? It means that every place that I touch Steve," I pause while tapping his chest, "you will feel it too!" Pam smiles. Everybody's laughing like crazy. "No, really," I say. "Let's take it to the next step." I lead Pam and Steve over to a couple of chairs and let them sit down.

"So Steve, I'm going to hypnotize you now. Without really knowing how to hypnotize. Cool, huh? I'm going to count to five and when I say 'five,' you will fall into a deep hypnotic trance. One, two, three, four, five. Close your eyes, you're hypnotized." Steve has a huge grin on his face.

"Those of you who don't believe that Steve is now hypnotized please raise your hand." Many hands shoot into the air. I raise my own hand. "As you can see I raised my hand too." Laughter. "Okay, now, if you do believe me, raise your hand." A couple of kindhearted people—or clowns—raise their hands. "Thanks, Mom." I move away now from Pam and Steve to the other side of the stage. "To show you that Steve really is hypnotized I'll stand over here. Steve, please open your eyes and look at me." Steve does so. "You see, like a robot, he obeys my every command." Steve is laughing now, trying not to, but shaking in his chair. I head back over to him and place my hand on his shoulder. "Now let me just cover your eyes with a blindfold." I slip the blindfold over him and pick something up from a small table on the stage. It's a fork. A big one. I hold it in my hand and stand behind Steve. "Tell me," I say to him, "have you ever heard of Chinese acupuncture?" The audience roars with laughter at this. Pam, too. She has twisted around in her chair to get a better look. Steve smiles.

"Steve, I need you to point your finger at Pam, and Pam, you need to point your finger at Steve. Now be careful. The energy is going to flow from your hand to his, so don't point too low because I'm not responsible for what will happen." The room erupts into laughter. Steve looks a little nervous and shifts in his chair.

"Okay, ladies and gentlemen—I'm going to count to three. When I say three, I am going to . . ."—here I take the fork and pretend to stab Pam with it—"entertain you, and I'm going to ask you to clap your hands on three. Ready? One, two . . . three! Clap your hands!" Everyone claps their hands like crazy.

I lunge forward and jab Pam lightly in her behind with the fork. Immediately, Steve jumps into the air. He pulls off the blindfold in shock, then he and Pam just sit there laughing, shaking. The audience is on its feet with the excitement and energy. "Oh my god," I shout, "this means you are so connected. Give them a big round of applause!" The music starts up. Pam and Steve make their way to the steps, laughing and talking together.

"By the way, I have to tell you this: the pain will be gone in a month." Laughter. "And this hypnotic situation only lasts for a week. This means that every place you touch yourself in the next week—she will feel it also." Lots of laughter. "Oh, and Pam, if you feel something at two A.M., it's not me." I stand on stage watching the audience laugh, enjoying the moment. Then I grab the microphone, walk into the spotlight, and shout, "By the way, I almost forgot. Where is the money?" From his distant row, Blake yells, "THE MONEY IS HERE."

Let me read your mind for a minute. I want you to think of one of the six playing cards below. Make sure you remember the color, suit, and value. Think only of one of them and don't forget it. Do you have one? Great.

OK. Now I'd like to look deep into your eyes for a moment, so peer into my eyes in this photo of me.

Look away for a second, because I'm going to try to take away the card you thought of. Turn the page and tell me that I guessed correctly.

Your card is no longer there. Amazing, right?

Would you like to try one more time?

Take a look at these six new cards and think of only one.

Now that you've thought of one, remember to look deep into my eyes. Don't worry, I'll try not to hypnotize you. (Did you know hypnosis is illegal in Israel unless you're a doctor and have a special license?)

And now, prepare to be stunned again.

Your card is no longer there.

Pretty cool, right?

OK, so I'm guessing that by now you've figured out that this is not really a demonstration of my mind-reading abilities. I promise you I can do better than this! Instead I'm just showing you how sometimes our minds take shortcuts. The second group of cards I showed you doesn't contain *any* of the cards from the first set. Of *course* your card is missing. *All* the original cards are missing, so the trick works no matter which card you pick. Even though it's just a trick, it's still pretty fun. You can fool most people once, or even twice, but then they start to get suspicious and start to remember other cards from the first set . . . like you. Go ahead and show the trick to your friends and family and see their reactions.

Here the brain is being lazy—or super-efficient. It's taking in the cards in general, perceiving them as a group of royal cards or a group of sevens, eights, and nines without focusing on the specifics. Which is fine if you're watching a low-stakes card game, but not if you witness a crime and have to give details in court. Now go back to page 55 for some more brain games.

The Stroop Test

Say the **COLOR** the words are written in out loud. And I mean out loud.

1) GREEN BLUE ORANGE
BLACK RED GREEN
PURPLE YELLOW RED
ORANGE GREEN **BLACK**

Good job! That was pretty easy. Now do the same again with the second set—say only the **COLOR** the words are written in out loud, not the word itself. Try to do it fast . . . Ready? Go!

2) YELLOW BLUE ORANGE
BLACK RED **GREEN**
PURPLE YELLOW RED
ORANGE GREEN BLACK
BLUE RED **PURPLE**
GREEN BLUE ORANGE

Was it hard? That's because your left and right brain were in conflict. Now try the third set, again saying out loud only the **COLOR** the words are written in.

3) NVSLVSL MMIMOZ QGERDSTE
MCPSIKERB POKXRG LUKJO
DTYGROOP SPVJPUVB FREFRJ

That was much easier, right? Go back to page 188 and I'll explain what was going on in your brain.

DO YOU THINK YOU
YOU CAN FIND
THE MISTAKE?

1 2 3 4 5 6 7 8 9

Have you noticed that it has the word "you" twice? That's the mistake.

FIVE

Harnessing the Positive Power of Energy

I'm in a cool restaurant downtown, all glass walls and a well-stocked bar. "May I borrow your glasses, please?" I ask a young woman as I approach her table. She looks nervous, but takes off her glasses and hands them over to me. "What's your name?"

"Jennifer."

"Well, Jennifer, do you have insurance?" I ask. She shakes her head, her eyes wide. "You should have." Shock flickers across her face, then laughter. "Here, hold out your hands, palms up, and I'll put the glasses on them. They'll be safe that way. Just keep your hands flat and let the glasses lie there." Now I get serious. I focus on the glasses, rub my hands together, over the top of the glasses, concentrating my thoughts. The people around me are quiet, watching, waiting. I can sense them, but all my thoughts are on the glasses. Suddenly, the glasses leap into the air, flip over, and land neatly back in Jennifer's hands. She grins with amazement, and maybe relief. "Cool, right?" I ask.

A woman sitting at the next table says, "Can you do that with people?" It's a question I haven't been asked before, and for a second I'm silent, visualizing the woman turning a somersault six feet up. "Sure I can," I say and walk toward the woman. "What's your name?"

"Liz."

"Okay, then, Liz." I act as if I'm going to pick her up and hurl her into the air. Everyone laughs, Liz especially, although I can see she's nervous, wishing she hadn't asked the question. "So if you stand here and close your eyes, I'll stand behind you." She does as instructed, and I stand a couple of feet back, concentrating on the back of her head, the top of her shoulders. I put my arms out, not touching her but close, and then I slowly, slowly draw my hands back toward me. Liz moves, too, her shoulders following my hands, her feet not moving, until her whole body is leaning backward. "You feel it?" I ask. She nods, eyes still closed. She's tilting backward now, leaning like the Tower of Pisa. "Stop it," she shouts. "Are you touching me?" "No," I say. "Stop pulling me!" Her arms are flailing. I know it must feel strange, scary even. "There's no one touching you," I say calmly. But she's moving her feet now, getting herself upright. "Okay," I say. "Open your eyes." She spins around to look at me. "That was terrifying," she says. "I felt this weird energy, then I thought it was hands pulling me." She's laughing now, shaking with nervous energy, which makes everyone else laugh. "That was amazing," she adds, and goes back to her seat.

"How do you do that?" Jennifer asks.

"Energy," I say. "Chi energy, positive energy. I control it with my mind. With your mind too."

The term "chi" is Chinese, but you may have heard of *ki, chai,* or *prana.* These are the Japanese, Hebrew, and Sanskrit words for "energy" or "life force." It's the natural energy in the universe that makes up everything. I like to think of it as positive energy, and I practice it during my performances and in my life offstage. It exists both inside and outside our bodies, and the more we are able to harness and draw inside ourselves, the more energetic and vital we are.

As a huge fan of the *Star Wars* movies, I've always been interested in the connection between chi and the Force. As Obi-Wan Kenobi says to Luke Skywalker, "The Force is what gives a Jedi his power. It's an energy field created by all living things. It surrounds us, penetrates us, and binds the galaxy together." Sounds like chi to me.

The Chinese have a saying that "chi follows *yi,*" where *yi* is the mind or intention. This phrase relates exactly to some of the skills I use as a mentalist. When I focus my mind, energy flows in that direction. The more I focus, the more energy flows. In fact, I can specifically focus on having the energy flow to where I want it. You can try this by thinking about a part of your body, your foot maybe, or your hand. Really focus on it and become aware of it. Imagine the way the veins are trembling just below the surface of the skin, the way blood is flowing through your veins, carrying its life force with it. Now imagine the blood as energy pumping through your body. Maybe you'll feel a tingling in your foot. Maybe it will start to seem a bit warm. That's the sensation of energy.

So how do I use this power to influence the world around me? Although I didn't know it at the time, I was focusing the chi, my internal energy, when I was that six-year-old boy playing with my food and making my spoon move across the bowl. Back then I was only able to move the spoon a fraction of an inch and only some of the time—so most of our family meal times progressed peacefully enough—but now, after years of study and practice, I am able to focus a large amount of this energy whenever I wish.

When I want to bend a spoon or nail or the stem of a wine glass, I have to focus very hard, use my mind to summon this energy from inside me and direct it at the spot I intend to shape. Again, the image of the laser beam is useful here for explaining what is going on. It is not enough to hope that the spoon bends or to merely want it to bend; it is a matter of willing it. I shout, "Bend, bend," in my mind as I'm using my mind to summon up, control, and project my chi energy. This is the basis for telekinesis—moving an object or changing its form by using the power of the mind. I move back and forth between bantering with the audience and intensely focusing on the object. It takes a lot of effort. When I'm working on bending an object, first it becomes warm with the high level of kinetic energy before we see it begin to soften and bend. It can be exhausting. When I make watches stop and eyeglasses spin through the air, this still requires a lot of focus to generate enough energy, but not as much as for bending silverware.

Sometimes I'll ask the audience for help by inviting a group of people up on stage. I ask them to stand around me and support me. In this way, I can use their energy levels to increase the flow of positive energy. As a bonus, it makes the act more interesting when people see the object changing right before their very eyes. I'll also put a piece of silverware or a coin into someone's hand and send the energy through them to the object. In this way, it's clear that I'm not physically manipulating the object in any way—it's all mental. This always makes a very strong impression.

CAN'T WAIT TO SEE ME BEND SOME SPOONS AND COINS AND MOVE EYEGLASSES WITH THE POWER OF MY MIND? THEN GO TO

WWW.MINDREADERBOOK.COM/ENERGY

Remember Pam and Steve on stage just now? I've done this same act many times with people who know each other, husband and wife, or friends, but not always. I've also performed it with some interesting celebrity pairings, including Jay Leno and Zac Efron on my first appearance on *The Tonight Show,* and Arnold Schwarzenegger and a Los Angeles rabbi.

The way that I transfer sensations of touch from one person to the other during this part of the show is by using the power of chi energy. First, I'll blindfold one person and tell them that I'm going to touch them somewhere and, when they feel the sensation of touch, they should let me know. Then I'll tickle the other person on the chin or gently touch their nose. Or so it seems. Really, I'm sending the chi energy from one to the other, as I did with Pam and Steve. The sensation is very strong for the person not being touched. They're always amazed when I tell them they haven't been touched at all. The audience always loves the look of amazement on the participant's face. "But I felt it!" they say, astonished. The power of chi energy is very strong.

Once I gave a show in Israel and one of the participants on stage was an Orthodox Jew. She was concerned about being touched by a male, as it was against her belief, and I assured her that she wouldn't be touched. Well, of course, with the transfer of energy she felt the touch, and was very upset. I told her she hadn't been touched at all. The audience told her she hadn't been touched. But she wouldn't believe it. Not until she saw it replayed on video. Then she believed me and was astonished.

Although this transfer of energy is exhausting for me, both mentally and physically, it produces positive energy in the audience, which, in turn, keeps me energized. The energy cycles around the theater from me to the audience and back. The more they enjoy the entertainment, the more good energy there is.

There's something very exciting about standing on stage in front of a large audience and feeling them respond to the things

I say and do. As so much of what I do relies on thought persuasion, I feel like it's almost my duty to persuade people to feel happier, to experience positive thoughts. Everything I do comes from a good spot inside me. I can sense a buildup in positive energy in the audience as I get further along in my act each night. Sometimes an audience can be reserved in the beginning, still caught up with their thoughts and worries from their daily lives, so I have to work with them, channel their mood, and get them to focus on me, on the show. There'll be certain areas of the audience that warm up to me first, and as they relax and laugh, their neighbors will, too, and the good feelings will radiate outward. I often go out into the audience to make sure that the positive energy has reached the people in the back, so that they feel as connected as those in the front seats. Mostly, the energy is contagious. Once I've won one group over, then it will surge across the whole audience, some nights faster than others, but once it's there, it stays. All that positive energy is hugely powerful. In the preceding chapter, I talked about the importance of the emotional connection between me and the audience and the way it affects my ability to persuade, influence, and control. As you can see here, the positive energy builds into that, too. The more energy I can harness and inject into the audience, the more energy I have to work with throughout the performance—and it just keeps building.

After a show, my energy levels are very high and I feel as if I could really do anything I put my mind to. I'm Superman again! These are some of my most creative times. My mind is buzzing with ideas and it's when I come up with many of my new ideas for shows, or books, or iPhone applications. All that energy produces a positive mind-set, so I can think about anything as a possibility. I come up with so many "what-if"s when I'm in this state. My friends and colleagues are no longer surprised to get lots of frenzied e-mails from me in the middle of the night.

The audience leaves my shows with this sense of positivity, too. I'm always very happy when I feel how much an audience has enjoyed the show. My show is not like some of those shows or plays where you leave the theater completely drained and mentally exhausted, and need a couple of drinks to make you feel human again. I've heard from so many people that this general upbeat attitude, this feeling of well-being, lasts for a long time after the show, especially as people connect further by talking about what they've just experienced.

I try to radiate positive energy in every direction, wherever I go. One of my favorite things to do is get people to say "wow," and to make them laugh. What could be more positive than that? Whenever I amaze people—whether it's in an informal setting on a beach or a street somewhere or at a live show—I love to see the wonder on their faces. It's like they're little children again. Some people, of course, ask me questions and try to rationalize what I do, or they tell me they think it's all tricks and fakery—which, by the way, I don't mind. I always ask them, "Did you enjoy the show?" and when they say, "Yes, it was amazing," I know I've done my part. That's all that matters. It's not for me to turn nonbelievers into believers. My hope is that people enjoy the entertainment that is at the core of everything I do. I think I can say that nearly everyone leaves one of my performances feeling very positive. I agree one hundred percent with Charlie Chaplin, who said, "A day without laughter is a day wasted."

Ever since I started performing as a mentalist, I've had a catch phrase, a motto, printed on postcards and business cards, and it sums up very well two elements of my show. "Always think happy thoughts, as you never know who's reading them." I'm a big believer in thinking positively. If I can harness enough energy with my mind to move objects, to make solid objects bend, to send a jolt of energy from one person to another, then it's clear that our minds have the capacity to affect the world around us. It's up to us to use that energy in a positive way, to channel our chi to create a wellspring of positivity in us that overflows into our daily lives.

I draw inspiration from many sources, and when I was told this story that I'm about to tell you, it made me so happy, so energized. It's one of my favorites about overcoming negativity and channeling it into positive thinking with amazing results. A man called Ferruccio (1916–1993) grew up in a farming family in Italy but found himself more interested in farming equipment than the agricultural side of the business. After working as a mechanic in the Royal Navy, he founded his own tractor company. His company did very well, becoming the best in Italy, and through his hard work Ferruccio was able to buy several nice cars for himself, including the car of his dreams—a Ferrari. He loved this car but found it had problems with the clutch, and so he would drive it over to Maranello to have it serviced at the Ferrari factory there. Each time, the mechanics would take the car away and fix it in secret—which annoyed

Ferruccio. After several such experiences, Ferruccio met with Enzo Ferrari himself to talk about the problems with the clutch, but, the story goes, Ferrari did not like the impudence of the "tractor driver" and told him, "Nobody will tell Enzo Ferrari how to build cars." So Ferruccio decided he would build his own car, one with a properly working clutch, one to rival and beat all Ferraris. Which he did. And he gave the car his family name: Lamborghini.

Doesn't that make you think about times when someone has treated you badly and make you want to go back in time and turn the negative energy into positive energy? We can't do that, of course, but we can try to focus on increasing the positive energy around us in the future.

One of the mind-reading acts I like to do involves asking someone to draw something while I leave the room—and then I try to draw the exact same shape. What's funny is that most people draw a smiley face. So much so that now I specifically ask people not to draw them, so that I still have a challenge. This kind of smiley, "have a nice day" way of being happy is so ingrained in Western culture that we say things and do "happy" things without really thinking about it. It's us operating on auto-pilot again. "Enjoy!" we say before eating, but again we don't really think about what we're saying. So, when I talk about positive energy, I don't just mean that. I don't mean reacting to life's events with happiness or sadness but trying to increase the potential for happiness, for positive experiences in our lives by increasing our chi energy. Our vitality.

Like most things, the chi energy in our bodies needs to be replaced and replenished as it gets used up, and to do that we have to pull in more energy from the world outside. There is a special way to do this and it involves focusing on our breathing. If you're like me, then breathing is something that you don't really think about most of the time—it just happens while you're thinking about other, supposedly more important things. But if you do pay attention to the way you breathe, then, most likely, you'll notice that you're breathing incorrectly. Most of us breathe in through our noses and out through our mouths, and our abdomens get sucked in instead of out. It's all completely wrong.

Pay attention to your breathing for a while. Breathe in oxygen and energy through your nose and down into your lungs and feel them inflating. Then breathe out through your nose with your mouth closed. This maximizes the chi entering your body and minimizes the amount escaping through your mouth. This method has two benefits: more chi energy in your mind and body, and a feeling of relaxation as you slow down and focus only on your breathing.

If we think of chi energy as a kind of life force (may the Force be with you), then it makes sense that it gives us a sense of vitality, of wanting to get the most out of our lives. When we allow this positive energy to combine with the power of our mind, then the result is not just a vague happy feeling but directed positivity. If our thoughts create our reality, or, at the very least, our perception of that reality, then doesn't it make sense that our thoughts should all be positive ones?

The Buddha said, "All that we are is the result of what we have thought. The mind is everything. What we think, we become." I really believe that and I'm not a Buddhist. So when we remember ourselves, our life story up to this point, it doesn't really reflect who we are today. Instead, it's who we were in the past. What we think about today will be our reality in the future, so it makes sense to think in positive terms.

We all know some people who seem to attract negative situations and end up with a lot of bad things happening in their lives. Others seem to have constant good luck and perfect, happy lives. Think about these different people's mind-sets. Is the person who attracts bad luck a grumpy, depressed kind of person? And the person with the perfect life a happy, positive kind of person? Now, it's easy to say, well of course she's grumpy, or of course she's happy—look at her life. But I bet you these people have always been this way—negative or positive—and have helped to contribute to their own "luck" or "fate" or whatever you like to call it. If you think in a negative way, then negative things will happen. It can be a terrible, debilitating, never-ending situation. Once one bad thing has come into your life then you're on a downward path, because you think you've earned the right to be negative. And guess what more negativity breeds? You're right. More negativity.

Every day when I work as a mentalist, I have to use chi energy to create a positive mind-set both in myself and in my audience. I can't go out on stage or to a party with negativity anywhere in my mind, as it affects everything I do. Negativity breeds doubts, and I have to believe that everything in my show is going to go according to plan. In my line of work, where mind has extra power over matter, it's even more important to stay positive. Sometimes being a mentalist is a bit of a leap of faith. I also need to use positive energy to create a connection with the audience. If I'm negative or half-hearted, then the audience will be, too. Confidence is very important in persuasion and focused positivity can be seen as a form of confidence. The more positive energy I give out, the more will come back to me, on and off stage.

I have worked very hard on the timing and pacing of my show—but also on the energy levels throughout. It's almost like I've developed a toggle switch where I ramp up the energy level, then bring it down again. I control it and manipulate it as needed. I'll show the audience something mind-blowing and then I'll throw in some humor. Then something amazing, then more humor. I keep working that switch, up, down, up, down, but always keeping the general mood up, working with all my senses.

The fact that laughter is contagious is something that works in my favor as an entertainer. But I don't really want it getting too out of hand. There are serious acts of mental focus that I perform that need a certain level of concentration from both me and the audience. So I have to control the laughter, keep it at a certain level of creative energy but not overflowing into chaos.

As you know, things don't always go according to plan in a show, and when that happens, the precious energy level is in danger of getting dragged down. For example, it can be so annoying when someone's cell phone goes off. This happens a lot with Israelis. Go figure. I'll be in the middle of an act, with the audience totally focused on me, and then that loud trill of the phone breaks into everything. *rring . . . rring . . .* I used to get so mad. But what could I do? Yell at the person? Tell them off in front of everyone like they're a schoolkid? Or have them hauled out by security? None of these would be very good for the positive energy of the show. So what I do now is I incorporate the ringing cell phone into the act. I even look forward to its intrusion.

The guilty person with the phone always looks so embarrassed as they're hunting in their bag or pocket for the ringing phone, while other members of the audience are giving them dirty looks, so now I say, "Don't worry. Go ahead and answer." The person looks relieved and surprised then answers the phone and the other people in the audience relax. Usually I'll go ahead and read the caller's mind——I'll guess their birthday or zodiac sign. Imagine their surprise! Everyone loves it. It's so unexpected. The positive energy level zips up even higher——and I get to politely remind everyone else to turn off the ringers on their phones. When I first started to do shows in the United States and Europe, I would wait for someone's phone to go off. But it never did. Everyone has been much better trained about their phones here! But it was such a good act that I wanted to have it in every performance, so I have the only show in the world that says "Please do not turn off your cell phones" at the beginning.

Another time the energy of a show can slide is if I get something wrong. I want to quickly add that I'm right about 92 percent of the time——pretty good, right?——but as with everything in life, once in a while something doesn't go quite according to plan. An audience can be thrown into a sense of unease at times like this. What should have happened? Was it their fault? Their mood can turn into embarrassment or pity instead of amazement. Because of this, my reaction to things going wrong is to add a bit of humor. This gets the energy pendulum swinging the other way—from negative to positive.

I've heard that medical patients don't sue doctors that they like. It's the same with performers. Audiences forgive the ones who know how to be funny about mistakes. I remember once I was trying to guess someone's first love and I asked if the person they were thinking about had blond hair. It was the image that came to me. The guy said no. So I made a funny joke out of it: "Well, she's probably dyed it since you last saw her." Everyone laughed and no one minded that I had made a mistake. I went on to guess the name anyway. When I was on the TV show *The Successor* and something went wrong, I would usually say, "Oh, I bet Uri would have done this better." It always brought a big laugh from the audience—and the judges.

Interesting, I've noticed that the surge of positive energy can be very high after something has gone wrong and I've handled the situation. Now sometimes I'll even pretend to get things wrong to keep that flow of energy moving. Toggle the switch on, off, ON. Once I asked two people to tell me three different numbers. They came up with sixteen, ninety-one, and forty-two. Next I asked one of them to make a grid of nine squares—three rows and three columns—and write the three numbers in three squares without showing me any of the squares. Their choice. The objective, I said, was for me to also write the numbers in my own grid and guess the exact positions of the numbers. When I showed my grid, it was completely wrong. The two people and the audience were disappointed and embarrassed for me. I paused, then said, "Oh well, it doesn't matter. This is what I really wanted to show you." And I handed over a lotto ticket with three silver squares for scratching off. "Go on," I said. "Scratch the squares and tell me the numbers." Of course, the numbers were sixteen, ninety-one, and forty-two. Everyone was completely blown away—more than if I'd just gotten my own grid right!

Speaking of mistakes, did you notice I just made one? Page 128 is missing. Were you paying attention?

Tokyo, 2011

I'm on a big TV show and I've asked a guest to think of a two-digit number and not tell anyone. Next, I show her—and the audience—a four-by-four grid of squares, sixteen squares in all. My job is to fill out all the squares with numbers in less than twenty seconds, and one of the squares will hold the guest's number. Simple enough. Ready . . . set . . . GO! I very rapidly complete all the squares, concentrating hard and writing quickly. When I finish, I hold up the completed grid in excitement with all its numbers for everyone to see. I ask the guest, "Is your number there?"

"No," she says.

"Are you sure?" I ask.

She says, "Yes."

"What was your number then?"

"Sixty-four." She's almost embarrassed to tell me. I sense uncertainty in the audience. Has the act gone wrong? How should they react? There is shuffling in the seats. It is time for me to put everyone out of their misery. Now for the fun surprise. Here's my filled-out grid:

Let's take a look. You remember that the guest's number was sixty-four. Well, every sum of every row is sixty-four. The sum of every column is sixty-four. The sum of the diagonals is sixty-four. The sum of the four corners is—you guessed it—sixty-four. The audience is screaming with laughter in surprise and amazement. People are shouting out more ways to get to sixty-four on the grid. Like the four numbers in the center. Or the two middle numbers in the top row and the two middle numbers in the bottom row. Everywhere they look, they can find sixty-four. I'm laughing, too, adding up all kinds of numbers to get to sixty-four, and harnessing all that positive energy as it surges through the TV studio.

SEE ALL THAT CRAZY ENERGY AT WORK
AS I PERFORM THIS INCREDIBLE ACT AT
WWW.MINDREADERBOOK.COM/NUMBERS

The Only Way Is Up

Are you an optimist or a pessimist? If you haven't guessed by now, I am definitely an optimist. I won't let pessimistic thoughts in, and I try to send them away any time they start to circle around me. Part of this is practice. I've trained myself to harness the positive with my mind. I remember an interviewer once asked me, "What if you don't succeed in America?" I just looked at him in surprise and said, "It's not an option." This is one of my main goals and I've always known that I will attain success in the United States. Thought of failure has never crossed my mind.

According to Tali Sharot, one of the most innovative neuroscientists at work today and author of *The Optimism Bias,* humans may be hardwired for optimism. The reasoning goes that we live with the knowledge of our own certain death and so we need to have the instinct to imagine good things, like a rosy future, to help us handle that knowledge. But how can we keep looking on the bright side when we have constant access to so much negative information, like tuning into twenty-four-hour-a-day news programs?

By scanning people's brains as they process both positive and negative information about the future, research scientists have discovered something fascinating. Our neurons encode desirable information that could boost our positive feelings but do not store sudden, undesirable information. So while our brains take note of a lucky lottery winner's good fortune and enhance our optimism by having us think that we, too, could be a winner one day, hearing dire news about job loss does not make us worry specifically about our place in the workforce. Sometimes it's easier to be optimistic about the general future rather than specific events. While we might be optimistic about earning more money next year, we might not be optimistic about getting a particular job after a job interview. Did you know that 10 percent of Americans expect to live to a hundred years old, whereas, in reality, only 0.02 percent live that long? Also, that 93 percent of Americans believe they are in the top-fiftieth percentile for driving ability?

How to Look on the Bright Side

Did you know that optimism is a learned skill? Most people think that you're either a glass-half-full or glass-half-empty kind of person. It's not true. Even the most negative people can learn a little optimism if they focus their minds on it.

- Change your tone of voice—if you speak "happy," you feel happy.

- Force yourself to be upbeat and energetic (there's that chi energy again!) to change your mood, your mind-set, and the people around you.

- Change the words you use to have more positive associations: in this way, "problems" become "challenges."

- Change the way you walk: take big steps, walk quickly with your shoulders back and head held high. Pessimists take slow, small steps and keep their heads down.

It might take some time to feel natural, but anyone can reprogram their mind and change the way they think about their feelings.

Here's a bit of cool brain science: in 1988, social psychologist Fritz Strack asked volunteers to hold a pen with their teeth—which created an artificial smile—or to hold a pen with their lips—which created an artificial frown. Later, the volunteers were shown funny cartoons and, you guessed it, those who had been forced to smile reacted more happily than those who had frowned. Make yourself smile and you'll feel more positive. Try it and see.

You've guessed by now that I'm a bit of a science nerd. I love learning about all the research that's been done about the brain and the mind. So, I was pretty interested when I found out that by channeling our energy into positive thoughts and behaviors, we can actually change the brain's biochemistry. Levels of serotonin, a "happy" hormone found naturally in the brain, get boosted when we have a positive mind-set. Doctors are always wanting to run tests on my brain to see the electrical activity in there—which, I'm sure, is crazy at times—and to see which parts light up when I'm bending spoons and reading minds. I haven't let them do that yet. But it's cool to know that every time I put on a performance I'm changing my own brain—and those of my audience.

In addition to higher levels of serotonin, neurologists have also shown through MRIs that happy people develop extra activity in the left prefrontal cortex of the brain. This is the part of the brain that handles positive emotions, like optimism. Compare that to those people experiencing anger, anxiety, and depression, which present as extra activity in the right prefrontal cortex. The higher the left-to-right ratio in the prefrontal cortex, the happier the person—and vice versa.

Lior's Guide to Meditation

It turns out that some of the happiest and calmest people in the world (other than sleeping babies) happen to be Buddhist monks. When a brain specialist, Dr. Richard Davidson, and his team, scanned the brains of monks, the activity in the left prefrontal cortex was crazily off the charts. But what was it about the monks' lifestyle that was making them so positive? Turns out it was meditation. Many research studies show that people who meditate regularly have very positive "left-to-right ratios" in their brains.

Why would meditation have that effect? And what is considered meditation? At its most basic, it's a way of taking time out of the day to be still, to focus and calm the mind, and to breathe. It's a time for replenishing your store of chi energy.

For me, the purpose of meditation is twofold: to get a sense of calm, and also to reenergize myself and my mind. It's a time when I don't have to think about specifics or plan anything or make decisions—it's like listening to silence. It clears my mind of all its chatter—and my mind has a lot of chatter. I think of my mind, my thoughts, as tools for the performances I give and the life I lead, so I need them to be in working order. If they are exhausted, they won't be good for anything—and that's not good for me. So, to me, it makes sense to spend five or ten minutes on meditation, whenever I can.

People who know me are often surprised to see me meditate, because usually I'm talking and thinking out loud and buzzing with energy. When they see me sitting, silent, eyes half-closed, they do a double take. But when they think about it, it makes sense. I'm taking a few minutes to spend with just my mind.

Meditation is a personal thing, so there isn't a right or wrong way to do it. But you also can't just tell someone to go and meditate and expect them to automatically know what to do. So here's what works for me. I find a quiet spot wherever I am—probably in a hotel room—and sit down, usually on the floor. I read somewhere that you have to meditate with a straight back, otherwise it's easy to fall asleep, so I try to keep my spine straight.

Next I close my eyes and try to silence my thoughts and all the other distractions around me. Cars in the street, the air-conditioner humming. This is much harder than it sounds, especially when you first start to meditate. I'm always amazed by how many thoughts I have at one time, fluttering around my mind. I find it helps to focus on my breathing, out through the nose, and while meditation is not supposed to be about multi-tasking, it's nice to visualize all that chi energy surging into the body. Thoughts flit into my mind and sometimes I'll follow a train of thought. When that happens, I throw the thought out of my mind—I read that somewhere—and refocus on the breathing.

Meditation makes me feel relaxed in an energetic kind of way—not like the relaxation of sleep. I feel very awake and open, my senses (all six of them) on alert. My mind feels very clear and still. I try to stay in this state of mental calm for as long as I can.

Most people are afraid to talk in front of a group of people, at work, at school, anywhere. So imagine how you would feel, standing backstage, knowing that in a moment you have to go on stage and speak to eight hundred people. Pretty scared, right? Now you understand why I've needed to find a way to relax.

For me, meditation is concentration. It's about centering myself, sitting in a room without distractions and putting my mind first. It's about having a dialogue with myself, asking questions—but not necessarily finding answers. Just finding a way to have a concentrated state of mind.

Even after a ten-minute meditation, I find my worldview has shifted radically. I'll feel more positive, more energetic, more in control. My thoughts seem less manic and more orderly, as if I have found solutions to worries without even knowing it.

Turning a Negative into a Positive

You might think that, as someone who is all about positive energy and happy thoughts, I consider skeptics my archenemy, with all that negativity threatening to ruin the positive energy I've built up during a show. Actually, no. I love a good skeptic. I love to prove them wrong. I've also learned from Uri Geller: the skeptics in his life have provided him with much free publicity and priceless exposure. He laps up everything that's written about him, good and bad, as he's aware that it all puts his name out into the world. As Oscar Wilde once said, "There's only one thing in the world worse than being talked about and that is not being talked about."

There's a quote by a magician called Hillel, which I absolutely love. He said, "There are two ways of living life. Nothing is a miracle or everything is a miracle, and you choose. If you want to be a skeptic all your life, you can be a skeptic all your life. I think being a skeptic closes many doors." It's so true. I believe in this so wholeheartedly. I'm not just talking about skeptics who doubt my abilities but people who are skeptical about life itself.

From the very first shows I performed at my friends' bar mitzvahs, I've had to deal with skeptics. Skepticism is universal. When someone is attacking what I do, calling me a fraud, it can be hard not to take it personally. But it also gives me a great opportunity to turn their negative energy into something positive. I'll make skeptical audience members part of the act, asking them, "So, do you believe in me yet?" throughout the show. It's a fun challenge to turn a skeptic into a believer. Skeptics are interesting as a psychological type, especially the ones who are so vociferously closed-minded. One of the things I love to do during my live performances is to bring a skeptic up onto the stage. Once I've guessed the name of their first teacher, or first love, they're blown away—and usually very quiet. Remember Professor Ootsuki in Japan? He was a big skeptic. Until he saw the newspaper act. Then I managed to guess eight out of ten digits of his personal phone number, and he was pretty impressed.

Geneva, 2009

Not so long ago, I had a situation that could have gone very badly. In this case, it wasn't with skeptics—it was with negativity and fear from the outside world.

I was in Switzerland, putting on a performance for the watch company Tissot, and I had a great show planned, with lots of watches starting and stopping all over the place. Anyway, I started up with my introductory banter, saying I was from Israel, a beautiful country that everyone should come and visit. As soon as I said this, three men stood up, exploding with anger, and started to walk toward the exit. I was really surprised. I'd never had anything like this happen before and I didn't want to ruin the start of the show by saying something negative. My mind was whirring. What should I do? I decided to shout out, smiling, "Excuse me. The standing ovation is usually at the end of the show." The audience laughed but the men did not. Their body language was super negative. One of them turned around and said they were leaving because I was from Israel. So, at least it wasn't personal. It turned out they were anti-Zionists from Dubai, who had political issues with Israel. They were furious. They continued toward the exit. The audience was watching them, whispering, and suddenly politics had entered the auditorium. The energy levels were moving down.

I decided to call out, "Please, do me a favor, before you go, think of a number between one and one hundred." One of them stopped walking and agreed, and, of course, when I asked him to say his chosen number, it was the one I had just written down. Luckily, the man laughed. His friends laughed, too, and relief swept through the audience. The three men sat down again and enjoyed the show with everybody else. It was a great show, a hugely positive show. After the energy levels went down, they went up higher than ever. When the performance was over, I went up to the three men, introduced myself, and we ended up in the bar with whiskey and cigars, talking and talking and talking.

That moment made me feel really proud, because it wasn't my special skills at work then. It was knowing how to focus on the positive and to transfer that energy to others. I felt like I'd done something really important for international relations—on a small scale, true, but still really important for the four of us. I'd reached out and the men had responded. I'm friends with them still, and hope to visit them one day in Dubai.

And now that you're feeling very positive, maybe you'll let me indulge in reading your mind? Just follow these instructions carefully.

Choose any two digit number between 10 and 99. Don't tell anyone. Add together both digits of your number and then subtract your answer from your original number. For example: choose 28, add 2 + 8 together = 10. Subtract 10 from your original number, 28, and get 18. 18 is your final number.

So go ahead and choose a number and do the math. Do you have a final number? Great. Now, I don't know if you noticed but each of the page numbers in the book has a symbol next to it. Go to the page number that matches your final number, and look carefully at the symbol. From now on this will be YOUR symbol, so put it in your mind and don't forget it. I promise we'll get back to it later in the book. Guess what? I'm going to read your mind. Now you can continue reading.

SIX

Trust Your Intuition

The intuitive mind is a sacred gift and the rational mind
is a faithful servant. We have created a society that honors
the servant and has forgotten the gift.

—ALBERT EINSTEIN

Have you ever had that experience of a song running through your mind and you turn on the radio and the same song is playing? Or you think of someone, and then they e-mail you? Or what about that moment when the telephone rings and you know who it is before you answer the phone? Everyone has experienced this: it's called "caller ID."

But, seriously, intuition has always played a big part in my life. Even when I was only about four or five, my mother noticed that I frequently seemed to know what she was about to say to me. And I don't mean just, "Go to your room, Lior." Often she'd be thinking about something, and then I'd ask her a question about it, although it was unrelated to anything that was going on around us. Or I'd come into the kitchen and she'd tell me some news, and I'd nod my head and say, "I know." I am sure it was a little weird for her, especially at first, but it was part of who I was—and still am—and so I didn't think too much about it.

I also always knew when people were lying. Back then, I hadn't read any of the books I've read now about body language and facial expressions and eye movements. Back then I just knew. It was a gut feeling. In the same way, I'd know immediately if someone could be trusted. Sometimes I'd think about someone I hadn't seen in a long time and then, the next moment, they'd be walking around the corner. Maybe someone's face would pop into my mind and the next thing you know the phone rings and it's them on the other end. Or I'd have a song playing in my mind and when the radio was turned on there was that song again. Things like this have happened to all of us, all the time. Even without caller ID. But for me these intuitive moments were constant: eight, nine, ten times a day, every day.

So, what do I mean when I use the word "intuition"? Basically, I think of it as a way of knowing something without going through the process of conscious reasoning. Knowing without knowing how you know. Reaching a conclusion without a logical reason for why. It's the kind of insight and information gained not just through the everyday use of my five senses but through an unconscious collaboration of all six senses. Intuition gives me the ability to be aware of, and tap into, wider areas of information and communication, and it's what guides me in making accurate predictions and choices.

Intuition is a part of cultural experience in many places around the globe. Native Americans search for and speak with spirits from nature. The Iroquois see their tribe as one body, regarding the scouts sent ahead of the tribe as eyes and ears that send intuitive pictures back to the rest of the tribe. My feeling is that in developed societies, we have lost our sense of intuition in two ways. First, we have evolved with a tendency toward the rational—if we can't explain it, we're not interested in it. Second, most children are quite intuitive when they are born. They are open to everything and unaware of where they, as individuals, end and the rest of the world begins. As they grow older, they see the values that society places on the rational, the concrete, the tangible—and they learn to dismiss intuition, instead embracing the "oh it's just a coincidence, it doesn't mean anything" school of thought. It's kind of sad.

Even the theory that women have a highly developed intuition is not necessarily true. It turns out that women are just better at reading nonverbal communication than men and so are more likely to pick up on emotional messages being sent by others, thus seeming more intuitive. But in research studies carried out by William Ickes, testing intuition in men and women, both genders fared equally—unless women were told their empathetic awareness was being measured, in which case they remembered the stereotype about women and intuition and performed better than men!

Still, even though we are less and less connected to our intuitions, we've all explained decisions using the words "I had a hunch," or "I went with my gut," or just simply, "I knew right away." Very often, when we have a hunch, we have a particular feeling in our bodies—like our body is sending out a signal. It can be very useful to recognize these signals and increase our understanding of what the hunch means. They are different for everyone.

How to Pinpoint Feelings

Think about something or someone that you really detest.

- How does it make you feel? Is there a sensation in your body that alerts you? Where? What is it like?

- Do you have an image of it in your mind's eye? What is the image like—a single frame, or continuous images like a movie? In black-and-white or color?

- Talk to yourself—in your mind—about not liking this particular thing and note the tone of your voice, the rate of your speech, etc.

Now think about something that you really enjoy.

- Notice the sensations you get in your body, and how they are different from the "dislike" sensations.

- Visualize the thing in your mind's eye and talk to yourself about it. Note any differences.

Now that you know your own body's baseline for its likes and dislikes, things that seem right and things that seem wrong, notice and act upon those signals.

Intuition plays a big role for me when I'm reading minds. When I tell someone I'm going to guess the name of their first love, they start sending out signals as soon as they think of the name. Some of these can be read as body language, but some of the signals are from their mind. Sometimes I'll see pictures, an image, or a letter. Sometimes I'm not sure what I see; it's just a feeling about a letter or a name. Just a hunch. This is when my intuition comes in. I use it along with my mental skills and my reading of the person's body language. As I ask the person questions about the name, I'll see and feel more from the new set of signals they send out. It's a little like a chess game, like breaking a code. Sometimes I'll get the whole name right away without any questions. This, I think, is true intuition. The name arrives in my mind like a feeling. Then I'll confirm it, step by step. Other times I'll get mixed signals and I have to make a choice, go with my gut, and ultimately use my intuition to make a decision.

Last year, I was the emcee at a big event in Los Angeles. I wanted to guess the name of someone's first love, and Mayor Antonio R. Villaraigosa stepped up and challenged me. He was very excited. He had a name in his mind that he was convinced I could never guess. I went through the questions with him, saw letters, but none of it was making sense.

I wrote the letters down and looked at the word. Was it even a name? My intuition was strongly telling me I was right, but my rational brain was questioning. I asked the mayor for the name. "Aurora," he said. I held up my cardboard with the name "Aurora" scribbled down. I was right. I hadn't even known the name existed, before this.

Intuition is not very well understood. Science has peered skeptically at it and—sadly for me—there is little true research on the subject despite the huge number of stories and anecdotes that seem to confirm its existence. And I don't just mean for me! I can guarantee that you or your friends have experienced at least one example of intuition at work:

- Feeling that someone is staring at you—and turning around to find that it's true

- Waking up a few moments before the alarm goes off—no matter what time you have set the alarm for

- Sensing that someone you know is in distress or danger

- Acting upon a sense of foreboding—and later finding out that it was well-placed

- Knowing what someone will say before they say it or completing someone's sentence

- Calling someone just as they're calling you

- Dreaming about an event before it happens

Very little of the evidence about intuition has been doc-
umented but consider these statistics. The vacancy rates on
the four planes that crashed on September 11, 2001, were
extremely high. The planes that hit the Twin Towers were 74
and 81 percent empty. Only 64 of the 289 seats were taken
on the plane that crashed into the Pentagon. It seems like a
lot of people may have canceled flights that day. Based on
intuition? There are reports of people canceling tickets for the
Titanic for no other reason than they had a hunch, or a gut
feeling, that something wasn't right. In fact, someone docu-
mented railroad accidents in the United States in the 1950s
and found that trains that had accidents had many fewer pas-
sengers than those that didn't. Sounds like more hunches and
ticket-canceling to me.

Here's a question for you.

Have you ever experienced déjà vu?

Here's a question for you.

Have you ever experienced déjà vu?

Over the past few years, I have taken on several work
assignments where my main role has not been as an enter-

tainer. Instead I've been asked to use my mentalist skills in other ways. I've been hired by politicians, celebrities, and businesspeople—for reasons of privacy, I can't give any names—to sit in on meetings and give feedback on the people in the meeting.

Private & Confidential, 2010

Mr. ████ and Ms. ████ have invited me to a meeting. I'm in a conference room in a modern high-rise building in a capital city. Floor-to-ceiling windows and the vibrant modern art centered on the bright walls give a feeling of light and optimism. Seated around the polished white conference table is a group of businessmen and businesswomen, all well-dressed, highly intelligent, and experienced. They chitchat awkwardly over binders bristling with important-looking papers. A graceful woman with bobbed gray hair introduces me around, and I smile enthusiastically and shake some hands. I ask a man wearing a dark blue tie to think of a number between one and one hundred. He frowns up at me, surprised but not happily so. The woman next to him laughs lightly and says to him, "Maybe you need another coffee?" He smiles with thin lips. "I'll do it," the woman says to me. "I love this kind of thing." After a few demonstrations of my skills, the men and women seem more relaxed. Conversation flows more easily. They laugh. One of the women calls me the official ice-breaker. The meeting begins and I sit at the end of the table, listening, nodding, and contributing an idea now and again. When the meeting ends, everyone shakes hands and leaves the room. Another business meeting over.

Except I stay in the conference room, thinking, looking out over the busy city below. In my mind, I am replaying the meeting, going through the sensations in my gut, rereading my scribbled notes. My purpose in the meeting was twofold. My visible role: break the ice and get the meeting off to a positive start. And then my invisible role: read the visitors inside and out.

My client wants to know whether she should consider investing in the visiting team's business proposal or stay away.

My job is not to give her business advice. It is to tell her my findings about the people at the table based on all my abilities combined—especially my intuition. I use intuition as a final reading on everything that my other five senses tell me. And today I have a hunch that someone at that table is incredibly dishonest. It actually makes me physically uncomfortable, because I don't think the other people in the group are aware of it. Of the six people who presented the proposal today, five are basically honest and believe in their product, and one person isn't and doesn't—and that person may drag the others down. I will inform my client so she will know.

When I give clients my assessment of a situation, I let them make their own decision on what to do with the information. Many times I have no idea whether they act upon it or not. But over the years I have also received follow-up phone calls, sometimes a year or two later, that confirm my thoughts. Nine out of ten times, in these cases, my intuition proves right.

For me, this sense of knowing comes from inside. Yes, my studies of body language mean that I can look at someone and maybe know more about them than the average person would. I've had a lot of practice and many opportunities to put it to the test. But the tipping point, the thing that makes me really sure, comes from inside. Every time.

The mind never stops impressing me as a powerful thing. Here, the evidence lies in its ability to process information and deliver it in so many ways that we don't even realize. Some ways we can rationalize and some we can't. I believe the key to using intuition is to use it in addition to—not instead of—the other five basic senses. For me, intuition doesn't just conveniently float through the window on its own. Instead, it arrives hand-in-hand with our conscious thoughts as an extra dimension that helps clarify and strengthen our purely rational thinking.

Maybe you know Malcolm Gladwell's book *Blink*. It's a book about instinct, about the way in which our brains think incredibly quickly to make decisions that can be just as good as decisions that are made after months of analysis and research. This amazing ability of processing information and arriving at the correct conclusion with only a brief amount of observation and without conscious awareness of the process is known as "thin slicing." For example, Gladwell tells us about a Greek statue that was correctly identified by some experts within seconds as a fake— although all the scientific testing and expert opinions compiled over months had suggested otherwise. Those who "just knew" the statue was a fake used thin slicing to make the judgment.

Gladwell doesn't like to use the word "intuition" when he describes this kind of decision-making, considering intuition to be emotional and irrational. He prefers the word "instinct," which he believes better represents thin slicing as a completely rational, speeded up thinking process. For me, however, I think that intuition goes one step beyond rational thinking. It is rational plus one. Five senses plus one. I embrace the power of my rational thinking to get in touch with my intuitive side. Only then do I consciously involve my intuition by asking questions of it to set it in motion.

Of all the acts of mentalism that I've performed, there's one that I've found that gets people really talking. That's sports predictions. I don't do them very often, as they're incredibly difficult and I can only do them when I feel them, not on demand. But I predicted the half-time score at an NBA basketball game, the

Sacramento Kings versus the Milwaukee Bucks. Before the NBA game, I wrote my prediction on a huge scroll of paper, and, in front of other people, locked the paper inside a cylinder inside a box, which was then taken away from me. The half-time score stood at Kings 48–Bucks 49. Before a crowd of twenty thousand people and filmed closely by TV cameras, I unlocked the box, took out the cylinder, and pulled out the scroll. Against a backdrop of much anticipation, I unrolled the paper to reveal my prediction written in big, black letters: HALF TIME SCORE: KINGS VS. BUCKS 48–49. The crowd went wild. I get asked about this one a lot. Is it an open prediction? How could I persuade two basketball teams to come up with this score?

Here's what my process was. I first visited both teams in their locker rooms and talked with the players, looked into their faces, and shook their hands. I also studied the statistics for each player. Once I had done all of this, I sat down and meditated a little and called on my intuition. Next, I wrote down the numbers 48 and 49. Once I had all the information I could possibly get about the teams and their players, I unleashed my intuition and went with my gut. But the important thing is that I allowed my intuition to be guided by my meticulous preparation. They worked hand in hand.

YOU CAN WATCH THE ENTIRE REVELATION OF MY PREDICTION AND SEE THE CROWD GO WILD AT
WWW.MINDREADERBOOK.COM/NBA

I have another act in development at the moment that uses some of the same principles. I haven't shown it publicly yet, but have practiced it a lot in private, and I hope to bring it to a TV show one day soon. Imagine a baseball player hitting a ball anywhere he wants on a baseball field. And then imagine me standing behind the player, holding a sketch of the field drawn on a white board. Two seconds before the player takes his swing, I place a cross on the sketched field, predicting where the ball will land. And each time the player hits the ball, and it goes straight to the place marked with a cross. That would be pretty cool, right?

I've worked on this back in Israel with soccer players kicking a ball into the goal and can't wait to try it with baseball. I use the same mental techniques as my NBA prediction, meaning that ultimately, after I've taken other factors into account, I use my intuition.

I was lucky to be born with a highly developed sense of intuition, but, equally lucky, I didn't ignore it. It was too interesting. Others might have said that everything was a coincidence. When people telephoned after I had just thought about them? Coincidence. Guessing correctly when someone was telling a lie? Coincidence. Guessing a number between one and ten and getting it right every time? Coincidence. The more we start believing in coincidences, the less we believe in intuition. As for me, I don't believe in coincidences. (Do you believe in coincidences? You do? What a coincidence.)

Develop Your Intuition

In my opinion, we are all born with intuition, and we all have varying degrees of it—even if we never listen to it. We just need to become aware of it, and to relearn how to use it. The more it is acknowledged, the stronger and more accurate it gets. So let's look at some ways to increase and develop our intuition.

- Believe in it. For your intuition to work, you have to acknowledge that it exists and that you are willing to take it seriously.

- Practice meditation. Or at least stop being crazy for ten minutes a day to let your intuition speak to you.

- Be open to the world around you. Be open to recurring situations and patterns with numbers.

- Take note of coincidences. As I always say, there are no coincidences—things happen for a reason.

- Question decisions and choices. This allows your intuition to engage with your rational thoughts. Don't operate on autopilot. Question, question, question. Remember, there are no stupid questions.

- Listen to what your body is telling you. Is your stomach tied up in knots when meeting with someone? Does something make you feel optimistic and energized?

- Recognize the importance of your energy level. If your energy is high in association with one choice, and very low in association with another choice, then take this into account.

- Take a few moments each morning to think about your dreams. Your subconscious has a lot to say, and makes much more sense than you may think.

- Take notes on when your intuition works for you—and when it doesn't. The more mindful you are, the better you'll become at recognizing and following your intuition.

- Be patient. Sometimes the results of your intuitive choices are not immediate.

Sometimes my intuition will step in during a show and make me change a whole segment, because suddenly I'll realize that the person I've picked for that part of the show is not quite right. With skeptics, for example, there are those who are willing to have their ideas challenged. These skeptics really want to see the proof of my skills so that they can believe in it. Then there are those who are completely closed-minded. If I made them levitate across the stage, they still wouldn't believe anything. My intuition will tell me which kind I'm dealing with, and whether it's worth getting them involved in my act. But, sometimes, my intuition on which kind a person is doesn't fully kick in until I've been interacting with them for a few minutes, and those are the occasions where I have to be really aware so that I know to change my approach.

When I was starting out as a mentalist, I had a lot of things to learn, especially about the way I presented my act. In the beginning, I would guess someone's number or a name and announce it to the audience. Then I would confirm it with the person. Sometimes they would deny it, and give another name or number so it looked like I'd given the wrong answer. It was bewildering and upsetting. I decided I would use my intuition to figure out who would be honest during the show and not change the name or number they'd thought about. That usually worked. But then I got really smart and asked the guest to give the answer first—for me to confirm. Now I just use my intuition when I really need to.

My intuition doesn't only come in handy during my shows. As a mentalist, I get all kinds of invitations to different events, large and small, private and public, in all corners of the world. It can be hard sometimes to work out which ones are the best to accept. I remember one particular case where the decision was almost impossible to make. I was in Germany, doing a bunch of shows that had taken a long time to set up and that were going really well. All of a sudden, I received a phone call from an American billionaire businessman. He was hosting a big event in Israel, and wanted me to perform there. The next week. But I was in Germany, and I was already booked to do another show on the night of the event.

As soon as I had a few minutes, I sat down to listen to my intuition. My rational mind had already weighed up the situation: I knew that going to the business event would be an important opportunity for me, and that it could lead to other opportunities. But I also knew that I had made commitments to the shows in Germany and I did not want to let those venues down—nor the friend who had helped to set up the shows there in the first place. My rational mind was thinking in the way we're taught in business management: with charts of upsides,

downsides, and conclusions. But every time I reached a conclusion, I started thinking about the problem again. I still hadn't
made a decision. My mind was whirling. That was when I
decided to listen to my gut feeling.

My gut was very clear on the matter. It said, "Go to Israel,
and do the show there." I listened again and still that feeling
was there. No swinging back and forth, no second-guessing.
My intuition was calm and resolved. I would go to Israel. The
interesting thing is that as soon as I had made my decision by
listening to my intuition, I was happy with it. I knew it was the
right thing to do.

The first thing I worked on was making sure I wasn't letting anyone down in Germany. I called a great friend of mine,
Amir Lustig—a fellow mentalist—in Israel and asked him if
he would handle my last show. He is a fantastic entertainer and
I knew that his show would be amazing, so I was able to tell
my German friends that I had found an excellent replacement
for my final show. And I was able to fly to Israel with a clear
conscience and meet the businessman—who later was instru-
mental in getting me my show in Vegas.

Things don't always work quite like that though. A couple of
years ago, I had the possibility of a big performance in New York
on New Year's Eve, for a huge amount of money. I was happy
about the idea. My managers loved it. But, for some reason, I
kept having this feeling that I should turn down the New York
performance and do something else instead. An important
German journalist had invited me to her house that evening to
perform at a private party—for no money—and I was convinced
that this was the right thing to do. I just didn't know why. When

I thought about it in a purely rational way, it seemed obvious that I should take the New York job. But every time I made this decision, I felt restless. At a deeper level, I knew it was wrong. And every time I asked myself rational questions about the decisions and then tuned into my intuition for the answer, I knew the right thing to do was to go to Germany.

So, against my managers' advice, I said no to New York. Instead I flew to Germany, taking a flight from Frankfurt to Berlin. And, as it was New Year's Eve, the flight was completely empty except for me, my two friends, my manager, the pilot, and the flight attendants. I have a photo of that empty plane. It would be a great story if I could say that I showed up at the party, did my performance, met some famous and fabulous people, and created ten opportunities for myself—all thanks to listening to my intuition. But the funny thing is that nothing happened. Yes, I did an amazing show, met some nice people, and had a lot of fun. But that happens a lot. Nothing else happened to make me understand why I went to Germany instead of New York that night. But I don't regret my decision. One day something will happen and I'll look back and say, "Now I get it. My intuition was right all along."

Just as I believe that our minds are more powerful than we can possibly understand, I also feel that almost everyone could improve their life by getting in closer touch with their intuition. It's an important part of taking ourselves off auto-pilot and really getting our minds to do the work they can. Intuition is one of those places where we're lazy, moving along like we always do, thinking that maybe we believe in intu-ition but not really doing anything about it. We'll think about intuition once in a while when one of those "coincidences" turns up and then we'll forget about it again. Instead, we need to get mindful with intuition. To call on it when we need it, and not wait for it to show up and tap us on the shoulder. I know that intuition definitely gets better with practice. So, I'd like to show you here two fun games to get into the habit of engaging your intuition.

Red Light—Green Light

- Imagine a traffic light in your mind. When you see the red light, think of the word "no." Now think of the green light, and think of the word "yes."

- Now you're going to apply the red or green light to questions that you ask yourself.

- Ask yourself some questions that have "true or false" answers, or "yes or no" answers, such as "Am I right-handed?" or "Do I like to eat sushi?" Take note of what color the traffic light turns in your mind's eye. Is it red or green?

- Next, try some simple statements and note the color of the traffic light again after each statement. "I live in Idaho." "I am a used-car salesperson."

- Now that you've tried the basics, see if you can apply some simple misdirection. Start by saying your name. ("I am Lior.") Then, call yourself by a different name. ("I am Peter.") Did the colors in your mind's eye change?

- Practice when you can, as it will help you to develop——and trust in——your intuitive skills.

- Try out your newfound skills in situations where you don't know the answer. Keep a note of your results, if possible.

Try a Blind Reading

- Sit down at a table with three blank index cards.

- Focus on a choice you are in the process of trying to make, and write down three solutions for the choice, one on each card.

- Next, turn over the cards so the writing is hidden, and shuffle them thoroughly. Place the cards next to each other, still facedown, on the table.

- Run your hands over the cards, touching them lightly with your fingertips, noting the feeling of each card.

- Assign a number to each card, based on how powerfully you're drawn to it. If you make the numbers total one hundred, so that each number is a percentage, it can be easier to compare the numbers.

- Turn over the card with the highest percentage—this will be your choice.

How did you do with these techniques? I have a strong feeling that your intuition is developing nicely.

Las Vegas, 2011
900 People

So here we are, back at my big show. I've done all kinds of mind-blowing things. Jane has chosen a number in a phone book that matched the number created by the women who mixed the cards; I've transferred chi energy; and Blake still has the $5 bill and the scroll. And no one has touched the money.

And now, from the middle of the stage, I shout, "Where is the money?" As before, Blake yells, "THE MONEY IS HERE!" He's been a great participant. "Well, now I need it here," I say. "Come on up." Blake is already halfway up to the stage, bounding up the steps, ready to assist. The audience cheers him, responding to his good-hearted energy.

"So, did anyone touch your money?" I ask.

He shakes his head, proudly holding up the $5 bill. I laugh. "Did I touch your money?" He shakes his head and exaggerates holding the bill far from me. "And you still have the scroll. Good. Now we're going to do something cool. Unfold the bill—but don't give it to me. Okay?"

Blake does exactly as he's instructed.

"Now, you took this bill out of your wallet at the beginning of the show, and you've held it in your hand since then?"

Blake nods.

"Could you please give me the scroll? I wrote something on it before the show." Blake hands it over and I slowly start to unroll it.

"Every bill in the world has its own unique, special serial number," I say to the audience. They're quiet now, attentive, watching my every move. "Blake, I want you to take a look at your bill and read out the serial number on it. Just the first seven numbers, please."

I hold up the unfurled scroll so everyone can see. There's a number written there. People in the audience are leaning forward now, their faces pulled toward the stage. Blake looks at his bill, finds the serial number, and starts to read. Slowly and clearly, he says, "Four six four nine six seven two." From the second number, people are saying, "No . . . No . . ." getting louder and louder, and by the seventh number the audience has gone wild. The number on the scroll matches the number on Blake's bill. People are clapping like crazy, turning to their neighbors, astonishment all over their faces. Blake is jumping up and down on the stage next to me, laughing and laughing with wonder.

I let the excitement continue while I put down the scroll, then I hold up my hand, grinning. "What are the chances of that?" I ask. "That I would predict the serial number on your bill?" People are still clapping. "But wait," I say. "You remember that Jane came up onto this stage and she chose a phone number at random from the phone book? And then the ladies over there chose the very same number when they mixed the cards? Well, that number is in the flip chart."

I go to the flip chart and start turning the pages. "Blake, what I want you to do is to read out the number that was the serial number on your $5 bill and that matched the number on the scroll please?"

As Blake reads his number again, loudly and slowly, I show the page in the flip chart with the phone number chosen by Jane.

Blake starts to read, "Four six four," but the rest of his number is drowned out by shouts from the audience. They can already see that the number on the scroll and the number on the flip chart are an exact match. The audience explodes. Everyone is on their feet, clapping, cheering, shouting, stomping, whistling. I'm being given a standing ovation that goes on and on and the show isn't over yet.

Next to me, Blake says, "How did you do that, man?" And gives me a high five.

SEVEN

Getting Creative with Thinking

*It should not be hard for you to stop sometimes and look
into the stains on the wall or the ashes in the fire or the
clouds in the sky or even mud, in which you will find
really marvelous ideas.*

—LEONARDO DA VINCI

When a well-known company wanted to fill a senior position,
they presented their applicants with this scenario as part of
the interview process: You're driving along, on a stormy night,
when you see three people waiting at a bus stop: an old woman
who appears to be on the verge of death, the man/woman of
your dreams, and a doctor you know who once saved your life.
You are allowed to take only one of them with you in your car.
Whom would you choose and why? Will you show mercy by
choosing the old woman, perhaps loyalty by choosing the doctor? A romantic nature by choosing the person of your dreams?
Or would you, in fact, be showing selfishness? So, whom did
the top applicant choose? The answer is . . . no one. He chose

instead to give his car keys to the doctor so she could help the old woman to a hospital while he waited for the bus with the woman of his dreams. So was the test really a personality test or was it a way to search for creative thinkers? How did you do?

There's an urban legend that I love, which goes like this: NASA spent millions of dollars to create a fantastic pen that writes in zero gravity, upside down, and in extreme temperatures—the famous Space Pen. The Russians just didn't have the same funding—so they used pencils . . . While the facts aren't true, the story makes you think, right?

I think a lot. I use my mind all the time, whether it's for persuasion, mind-reading, harnessing the power of chi energy, or invoking my intuition. I'm stopping watches and bending coins, guessing birthdays and first boyfriends, making people choose words in languages I can't even read. A question that a lot of people ask me is, "Do you think you use more than 10 percent of your brain?" It's one of those bits of brain science that people seem to like. When I was first asked this question, my response would be, "Yes, definitely. I mean, I can feel my neurons clicking away all over the place all the time." But then I began to think about it. Why do people think we only use 10 percent of the brain in the first place? Is it possible? Is there really 90 percent of the brain that we don't use, that we can tap into and become even more amazing? So I did some reading and it turns out that this idea is 100 percent myth. Brain researchers have shown that most of the different regions of the brain are continually active, and that we use all of our brain at some point every day. Of course, we don't use 100 percent of the brain 100 percent of the time. Some areas of the brain just hum along to keep us conscious while other parts of the brain get called into action during specific tasks.

But I couldn't stop thinking about this question. Wondering how much of our brain we use sent my neurons into overdrive. If science tells us that we all use all of our brain, that means that we don't have huge untapped areas waiting to be unlocked. At the same time, it seems to me that we don't always use our brain power well. Some people definitely tap in more effectively than others. As a mentalist, I've spent my entire life training my mind to work on specific mental tasks and I think I know pretty well how the brain and mind function. I've studied everything I can about psychology, the science of the mind, and how it relates to human behavior. I know how to focus, how to increase my chi energy to help the mental process, how to meditate. I think I use my mind's potential well. Still, there are days when I go through the motions in a brain fog. Days when I'm just not thinking. Or I'm distracted. Or tired. Days when I feel like I'm only using half my brain.

I'll give you an example. I've been invited to a private party to perform and I'm driving a rental car, looking for a parking space. It's been a tiring day in an unfamiliar city. I missed a lunch appointment because I got the dates mixed up, lost my hotel room key, and took three wrong turns getting to where I am now. I pull into a parking lot, finally find a spot, and zip in and park. As I get out of the car, I'm thinking about turning off the radio, grabbing my bags, and going through the evening's show in my mind. When I go to lock the car door, I find it's already locked—with the key inside. My heart sinks. No time to worry about it now though—I have a show to perform.

So how do you think my show goes that evening? You're probably guessing that I make mistakes, get my mind-reading wrong, forget people's names, and generally have the worst show of my life. Wrong. As soon as I step in front of the audience, my mind is sharp, focused, and aware. My show goes without a hitch. Only when I get back to the parking lot do I realize that I have absolutely no idea where I parked my car, much less how to get my keys back.

What's going on here? It's as if I'm working with two different minds. In the parking lot, before the show, I was distracted. I moved along using automatic reflexes. I did not actively engage my mind. If I had cut through everything else that was going on in my world, and said to myself, "let's focus," or "let's stop and think for a second," then I would not have left my keys in the car and I would have figured out a way to remember my parking space. This kind of "not thinking" goes on throughout the day, all the time. We all do it. Even you. I think maybe this is when we're only actively using a small portion of our brains, even though our brains are fully functioning.

Now let's take a look at what happened at my performance. Whenever I step out in front of an audience, I activate my mind to its highest level and consciously call every last drop of my brain power. My brain is fully charged to maximum capacity, ready to go. The key to using the mind's full power is to actively engage all of its resources, to crank up the "on" switch. To move away from the general light of the flashlight to the specific light of the laser beam.

Some people, though, seem to live their whole lives on

autopilot. Even when opportunities arise to engage their mind, they refuse to, and it's just something I have never understood. There's one story that I think about a lot when I encounter someone who refuses to open their mind.

I was very excited about going to work in America for the first time. It was a dream come true. My approval papers had been faxed through for my work visa. All I needed was an official signature and I would be good to go! It was hard to wait in line at the visa office. I felt like a kid, fidgeting with excitement. Finally it was my turn and I walked up to the windowed counter and handed over all my documents. I stood back, waiting for the clerk to look them over, stamp them, and unleash me.

"Excuse me, sir," she said. "Your visa has expired."

She pushed my fax back to me under the window, disinterested, ready to call the next person from the line.

"What do you mean?" I asked, mainly to keep her attention and my place at the window.

"Expired," she said, waving her hand at the fax. No explanation or elaboration.

I looked at the document, quickly scanning through it. Then I laughed. "Oh, I see," I said, sliding the fax back through to her. "The expiration date is next year, 2008. It looks blurred, but it says 2008."

The woman just shook her head. "Sir, it says 2006. Your visa has expired." Her lips started to form the word "next."

"No, really, it's 2008. Look. It was just issued last year."

She glanced down, a cursory look, her head already shaking. "I'm sorry, sir. It says 2006." Her tone was more forceful now. I could sense her heels digging in beneath the counter. This could go on for a long time. It was time to change tactics.

I reached for the fax and scanned it again. Exactly. I laughed. Charmingly, I hoped. "You see, here's the date of issue: 2007. So the expiration date can't be 2006. It doesn't make sense."

"Sir, it says 2006."

"And the issue date?"

"2007."

I laughed. It was really quite funny. "So let me ask you a question." The clerk looked at me, eyebrows raised, chin forward. Not the best body language for my case. "So, tell me, how is it possible that if the issuing date is 2007 then the expiration date could be 2006? Is it possible that we went back in time?"

I was hoping for a glimmer of a smile but all I got was, "Sir, I can't answer this question. The expiration date is 2006."

There was no point in going any further. I wished I could use my charisma and my powers of persuasion to get this woman to say yes, you're right, it looks like a 6 but obviously it's an 8. Here's your official stamp, and have a nice day. But her mind was closed tightly shut.

So I was left with two choices. I could call my father and ask him to refax a clearer copy of the form, or I could take a pen and lightly circle the blurred six to turn it into the eight it was. What do you think I did? Hint: this is a chapter on creative thinking.

The incident bothered me. It makes me crazy that people all over the world operate in the same manner without using their minds to think a little. It's like they're operating in a zone that doesn't have any logic to it, and definitely no intuition, or imagination, or creativity. No spark. They've been given very narrow instructions and if something appears beyond the scope of those instructions then they shut down. I can't answer that question. I haven't been programmed that way. We've all been given an amazing mind, a brain—why not use it as much as we can?

I've always been a huge fan of creative genius Leonardo da Vinci. Now there's someone who engaged 100 percent of his brain on a daily basis. While he's best known for his paintings, the *Mona Lisa* and *The Last Supper,* did you know he was also amazingly talented as a sculptor, architect, musician, scientist, mathematician, engineer, inventor, anatomist, geologist, cartographer, botanist, and writer? He created over thirteen thousand pages of detailed notes and sketches, and designed countless other inventions: the cannon, the machine gun, gliders, a turnspit for roasting meat, a canal system to irrigate fields and transport goods, the parachute, a movable bridge for the Duke of Milan, various ladders for storming and climbing castle walls, a machine to make concave mirrors, a pump for well water, a revolving stage, and an inflatable tube for floating in water. He's said to have invented the bicycle—over three hundred years before it appeared on the road! And he wrote in mirror-writing. See if you can read this.

One plus one doesn't always equal two.

Sometimes it equals eleven.

And just in case you don't have a mirror handy, here's what it says: "One plus one doesn't always equal two. Sometimes it equals eleven." It's an original Lior Suchardism. In other words, things are not always as obvious as they seem—sometimes we have to think laterally. We have to think around a problem or look at the same idea from two sides.

The human brain is capable of doing so much, and while I'm not saying that we all have the potential to be Leonardo da Vinci, I strongly believe that we all have the innate ability to do much more than we think we can. Let's get out of the box of narrow, constrained thinking and see what we can achieve. Let's be creative.

So, how about some brainteasers to get warmed up? Remember to think around the questions here and don't always go with the obvious answer. In other words, put your brain to work.

1. TWELVE PEARS HANGING HIGH, TWELVE MEN PASSING BY, EACH TOOK A PEAR AND LEFT ELEVEN HANGING THERE, HOW COULD THAT BE?

2. THERE ARE TWELVE MONTHS IN A YEAR. SOME OF THEM HAVE 31 DAYS. HOW MANY HAVE 28 DAYS?

3. WHAT BELONGS TO YOU BUT OTHER PEOPLE USE IT MORE THAN YOU?

1. Answer: One of the men was called Each.

2. Answer: All of them.

3. Answer: Your name.

Now you see there are many ways of looking at things! You have to stay on your mental toes.

One of the challenges for me as a mentalist is always keeping my show fresh, always using the new skills that I've developed. When I'm not on stage, I'm thinking, thinking, thinking about how I can improve my show. What can I do that I haven't done before? What no other mentalist has done before? How can I make my skills even better?

Now that I'm appearing on more talk shows, it's more important than ever to find ways to switch up my routine a little. I don't want viewers to see the same stuff each time! So, recently I was invited to appear again on *The Tonight Show with Jay Leno*. On my first appearance, I guessed which picture Jay would draw (a dollar bill), transferred chi energy between him and Zac Efron, and guessed a song that the band leader was thinking about. This, second time, I wanted to do something new and cool. But what? I sat down and thought about it, scribbling some ideas on paper just to get my mind focused and the ideas flowing. I couldn't think of anything right away, so I did this a few times. Nothing great sprang to mind at first, but I knew that now that I had actively started the process of looking for ideas, my mind would continue to generate them while I was doing other things.

A few days before the show, I learned that I'd be appearing with Kim Kardashian, and I decided that I would bring in a big pile of newspapers and predict which word she would choose from them. I had done this act before in many places. Remember Professor Ootsuki? But for this appearance, I wanted a twist. My idea was sparked by the word I knew she would choose. During the show, I gave Kim the choice of newspaper, the choice of page, and the choice of word. When I asked her which word she had chosen, she said, "Summer." This time, I hadn't written anything down on paper. Instead, I took off my jacket, and then my white shirt to show that underneath I was wearing a T-shirt. On the front, in bold letters, was written, I THINK KIM, and, when I turned around, on the back it said WILL CHOOSE SUMMER. She and Jay were blown away. It was such a bold idea. It clearly showed that I had predicted this word a long time before she set foot in the TV studio. It was also really visual and unusual. My idea had been sparked by the summer heat wave New York was having that week. Cool, right? And creative.

One interesting thing that I've found about adding new routines to my show, mixing them up a little, is that it's good for my brain. It was thought until recently that only children's brains were able to change and adapt, but that's not true. Brain scientists have learned over the past few years that it is possible to change the biochemistry of an adult brain. We already talked about the ways in which meditation and positive energy change the brain's structure. It also turns out that Buddhist monks who have meditated for many thousands of hours over many years have very high levels of gamma-wave activity in their brains, much higher than the average person. Gamma waves appear when different brain circuits connect and knit together, and are associated with a higher level of mental activity such as focus, memory, and learning. Just like any muscle, using the mind makes the mind stronger. I'd like to have my gamma waves measured one day.

Trying new activities and switching up our routines creates new neural pathways in the brain. That's easy for me—a no-brainer, you might say. I don't have a life with a lot of routine. My brain must love it when I jump on planes in the middle of the night to go to new countries and meet a bunch of new people. Whenever I try out new parts of my show, it also takes my thoughts down new and different brain pathways. Whenever we try something new, we're moved out of our mental—and often physical—comfort zone. We have to engage our minds to keep them strong. Remember when you learned to tie your shoes or ride a bike? You had to really, really concentrate—and practice—to get the job done properly. Doing that created new pathways in our brain, which, once we had mastered the skills, remained there for us to access any time we needed them. At that point, our thinking went from attentive learning to automatic, and the learning stopped.

Other small and easy ways to get your synapses flashing would be brushing your teeth with your left hand, learning a foreign language, taking up a new sport or hobby, wearing a blindfold for a while and getting around by touch. These have all been proven to give our brains a boost. You should try them sometime. Did you know the main reason that adults don't try new things is for fear of looking stupid? We'd rather sit on a couch and let our brains grow dim than look foolish in the eyes of others. Don't let that stop you. Don't be afraid to develop. Embrace the new, get creative, and boost your brain.

Another option for brain boosting comes from continued and deliberate practice of one particular thing. It could be a sport—this is how professional athletes get so good at what they do. Or it could be a hobby, like playing the guitar or chess, or knitting. I have spent my life practicing my mental skills in a focused way. Making connections in my brain and then strengthening them until certain parts of the act become automatic. In this case, I mean automatic in a good way, because it means that I can use what I had learned as a building block and go on to build another layer on top of it. Just as athletes practice their skills over and over again until they master them and can carry them out instinctively, then move on to the next level, continuously pushing at the edges of their comfort zone. In a similar way, my acts grew more complicated, more difficult. I still practice in this way. Whenever I have a new element in my act, it builds on mental skills that have become automatic and takes them to the next level. Then I practice it over and over again.

There's an amazing fact about London taxi drivers: They have a bigger hippocampus than most people—that's the part of the brain responsible for long-term memory, navigation, and making mental maps. To drive a traditional black cab, drivers have to learn and be tested on a crazy maze of streets around Charing Cross. It can take three years of training, and three-quarters of those who start the course give up. But those who finish are rewarded with real brain boosting—and higher pay.

How to Boost Your Memory

Remember my story about locking myself out of the car? There's an easy way to keep yourself from doing that. Use your left hand to lock up (if you're right-handed): the unusual action will fire neurons in your brain, create another level of consciousness, make you think about what you're doing and stop you from running on autopilot, so you'll remember it later. And, of course, this method can be used for other things, too.

As a mentalist, I've honed my memory skills, too, so I can easily remember all the different parts of my acts and so I can keep track of my hectic schedule. I like to use a memory system called the Peg System, to help me with lists.

To start, you have to memorize the peg words. Once you have these memorized, everything else becomes easy and they can be used repeatedly for many different lists.

Here are the peg words:

1. Gun
2. Shoe
3. Tree
4. Door
5. Hive
6. Sticks
7. Heaven
8. Gate
9. Line
10. Hen

Say them over and over until they are memorized. "One—gun, two—shoe, three—tree, etc."

Now when you want to memorize a list of items, you associate each item with the peg word to create a mental picture.

Imagine you have to remember a notepad, pencil, and spoon. Think of 1. Gun—notepad; 2. Shoe—pencil; and 3. Tree—spoon. Now think of an exaggerated or outrageous image to combine the pairs so that you will remember them. Maybe you're holding a notepad in your hand and a cowboy from the Wild West rides in on a huge horse, takes out a gun, and shoots a bullet straight through the notepad. That would make you remember, right? For the second one, how about you're walking along and your foot starts hurting, so you bend down and take off your shoe and dozens of pencils pour out. No wonder your foot was sore. Now, for number three, imagine you're sitting under a tree and you look up and see that instead of leaves the tree is hung with spoons. The wind blows and the spoons start raining down on your head. You get the picture.

It seems complicated at first, but once you've memorized the peg words, everything else fits easily into place. This method works because it creates associations in our mind. It's the same reason that no one can remember what they wore last Wednesday, but everyone knows exactly where they were or what they were doing on September 11, 2001. Our memories need a boost sometimes, a reminder to focus and remember.

The Whole Brain, and Nothing But . . .

Another brain question people ask me a lot is: are you a right-brained person or a left-brained person? Like the question about how much of my brain do I use, I first accepted it at face value. I would say that at school I was definitely a left-brained person, with my interest and ability in math and science, the subjects that deal with the rational and logical. I was also someone who read books with purpose, for gaining knowledge about psychology—again, this was a rational approach to learning. As I thought about it more, I began to realize that the way I read those books was not rational at all. The dipping into the back of the book, then moving forward and jumping around. Not sequential. And all that intuition I had. The constant losing of my keys. Maybe I wasn't so left-brained after all. Was I right-brained?

Realizing that the answer wasn't so straightforward, I took another look at the question that I had accepted without questioning. What did it really mean? Does the brain actually work like that? And, yes, I did some reading.

Not so long ago, the main thought in science was that the left side of the brain was the dominant hemisphere, in charge of rational, verbal activities such as speaking, reading, writing, mathematical reasoning, and all those other skills we're taught and taught at school. And the right brain was not so important. Then, in 1968, along came Roger Sperry's research on so-called split-brain patients—these people's brains were surgically cut for medical reasons, so they ended up with two separate hemispheres—and the studies came to some interesting conclusions. For example, when an image was shown to a patient's left eye, which is connected to the right-hand side of the brain, the patient would be unable to say the name of the object, because he couldn't access language centers in the left hemisphere. He could see the object but could not name it. However, when various objects were placed in front of him—

including the one he had just been shown—and the patient was asked to pick up the object he had seen, he was able to do so. Why? Because the right side of his brain had seen the object and could send a message to his left hand to pick it up. How amazing is that?

Sperry concluded, "Everything we have seen indicates that the surgery has left these people with two separate minds. That is, two separate spheres of consciousness." This research found specific differences between the two hemispheres and Sperry was awarded the Nobel Prize for his work. At the end of his acceptance speech, he said, "The great pleasure and feeling in my right brain is more than my left brain can find the words to tell you."

Take a look at what each hemisphere handles.

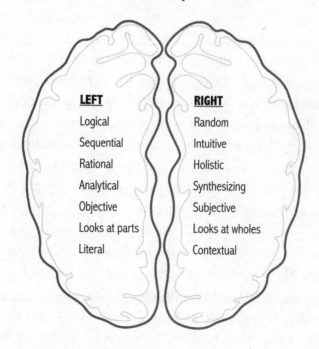

LEFT	RIGHT
Logical	Random
Sequential	Intuitive
Rational	Holistic
Analytical	Synthesizing
Objective	Subjective
Looks at parts	Looks at wholes
Literal	Contextual

Sperry had shown that the right side of the brain was as important as the left, and suddenly the right side of the brain became super-popular. We were all urged to get in touch with this newfound potential that had been locked away within our very own brains, undiscovered and under-nurtured for years. Left brain suddenly fell out of favor. It was a time for unleashing emotions and creativity. Schools were blamed for focusing on left-brain thinking. Standardized tests were condemned (but still used). A revolution of sorts was underway. Artists were in, accountants were out.

But it was a short-lived revolution. In theory, it was exciting to imagine a world where art and creativity, emotion and intuition were all-important. Wouldn't life be more interesting, more fun? But when it comes down to it, science doesn't really support the ideas of these two clear-cut sides to the brain. Humans are not either right-brain or left-brain types. It isn't as simple as that. And why would it be? We're dealing with the human brain here—the brain that built the pyramids, cured smallpox, and sent a man to the moon. The truth is that each side of the brain is better at handling certain kinds of information. The left hemisphere is in charge of sequence, literalness, and analysis, while the right hemisphere takes care of context, emotional expression, and synthesis.

You'll see what I mean when you've done the Stroop test, found in the photo insert section. The aim is to name the COLOR the words are written in, not to read the words themselves. Have a go at the first set and see how you do.

So, why is the second set so difficult? It's because the left side of your brain is trying to say the word it sees written down and the right brain is trying to say the color, so you have a tug-of-war between the two hemispheres. Only when the left brain has acknowledged that it needs to say the color can you get the job done. It causes some brain ache, right? We are so used to automatically processing words when we see them that it requires real effort to suppress that urge and name the colors instead. It's a good example of how we have to direct our attention and move from functioning on autopilot. And why is the third set easier?

Well, it's much easier when the meaning of the words doesn't get in the way, right?

So, back to the question of whether I am left-brained or right-brained. Like most people, I'm a bit of both. The two hemispheres of our brain handle different things but work together. We naturally use both sides of the brain for nearly everything we do.

Think back to me brainstorming about my appearance on Jay Leno. That was me using both sides of my brain. I sat down and thought rationally, logically about the fact that I needed something new for the show, and I wrote down a list of possibilities. Then I began to let my mind wander, make associations and connections that were not always logical, often didn't make sense. That was the right side of the brain slipping in—and in the end, it was the right side that came up with the idea of the T-shirt. Either way, creative problem-solving usually requires both analysis and sudden out-of-the-box insight. It's almost as if you go from narrow focus to wide focus and back again.

I've heard that when musicians improvise, they turn down activity at the front of the brain, as if to reduce their mental control and let their ideas wander. I've also always liked the image of Harry Potter author, J. K. Rowling, sitting on a train staring out of the window, when into her relaxed, intuitive brain came the boy wizard who would star in her bestsellers. But once he was in her brain, she had to switch to a different kind of thinking to work out her plot development and characterization.

We use both sides of the brain together all the time without even knowing about it. Imagine that you and a friend are throwing a surprise party. There have been a million things to plan—whom to invite, what food and drink to provide, where to buy it, etc., etc., etc. On your to-do list is, among many other things, "Buy ice." You know this, and your friend knows this. You work on the things you've agreed to handle while your friend works on her list. By seven o'clock on the evening of the party, the preparations are finished. Your friend decides to pour herself a glass of freshly made lemonade while waiting for you to finish your shower before the arrival of the first guests. She opens the freezer. No ice. "Where's the ice?" she shouts to you. In the next room, you turn off the hair dryer, and run into the kitchen in your bathrobe, a look of horror on your face, a hand over your mouth. "Fine, I'll get some ice," she snaps, slamming her glass down on the kitchen counter, snatching up car keys, and flouncing out the back door. You are in no doubt about your friend's state of mind at that moment. Just as she was able to figure out your answer to her question—"Where's the ice?"—even though you didn't utter a single word.

Here the two hemispheres of your brain—and your friend's brain—are working together very efficiently. The left hemisphere processes the literal meaning of the words "Fine, I'll get some ice," following rules of vocabulary and grammar. In fact, if only your left hemisphere was functioning, then you would hear those words and interpret only their literal meaning and understand only that your friend was going to go out and get some ice. But, because you have your right hemisphere to help you read some of the other nonliteral cues, you are able to understand that your friend is very angry with you. The right hemisphere of the brain is responsible for something called prosody—the rhythm, stress, and intonation of speech—and so it notices your friend's emotional state when she speaks, the sarcasm of the word "fine," her emphasis on the word "I'll." Throw in a little interpretation of the negative body language and you know exactly how your friend is feeling. Having used both sides of your brain to interpret the details of the words and the big picture of your friend's mood, you decide to finish getting dressed quickly, light a few candles, and hope that the guests arrive soon after your friend comes back with the ice.

This is your brain in action, using both sides together beautifully. But if you compare the party example to me using my brain during my mentalist act and during my brainstorming session, you'll see there's a difference. A big difference. With the ice for the party, you see the two sides of the brain working together automatically. This is what the brain does naturally and it's really good at it. During my act and my brainstorming session, I'm doing something else. I'm consciously drawing on both sides of the brain. There's a kind of thinking—a mindful way—that understands the power of the two sides of the brain and seeks it out. A lot of my act is completely rehearsed and practiced in a sequential manner (left brain) but then I have to be able to be spontaneous and creative in my thinking as the unexpected occurs (right brain). I use humor (right brain) but often some portion of the humorous content has been planned (left brain). I rely on intuition (right brain) but I actively engage my intuition to make decisions (left brain). I think in terms of the whole show and its progression (right brain) but I also focus on the details of each segment (left brain). I'm toggling back and forth the whole time, trying to use every last ounce of brain power, working the two hemispheres to get the most out of each other.

I find it's important to think about this, as we live in a world where rationality and logic are king. Most of us fall into left-brain thinking more than we should. We often choose carefully considered logic over intuition. We're constantly encouraged to do just that. We choose to play by the rules instead of bending them. We become comfortable inside the box. Instead we need to get out of that box and think with an open mind, be aware of what's around us, be receptive to new ideas and challenges. In essence, we need to bring the skills of our right hemisphere into play, too, and think with our whole brains. Now see if you can conjure up some whole-brain thinking to try the challenges here:

What would you do if I gave you a candle, a cardboard box of thumbtacks, and a book of matches, and asked you to attach the candle to the wall so that it did not drip onto the table below? These are the only materials available to you. Think about it. And I mean, really think.

How did you do? If you're like most people you thought

about melting the candle and sticking it to the wall without success, or fixing it to the wall with a tack. Even if these methods were to work—which is doubtful—would they stop the wax from dripping? The only way to solve this problem is to think outside the box—literally. Don't think of the box holding the thumbtacks as a box—think of it as a candleholder that can be tacked to the wall. Now it makes sense, right? This classic experiment is called Duncker's candle problem.

Now, see if you can wrap your brain around these lateral-thinking problems. Remember that famous quote, "One plus one does not always equal two . . . ?" You may need it here.

1. A murderer is condemned to death. He has to choose between three rooms. The first is full of raging fires, the second is full of assassins with loaded guns, and the third is full of lions that haven't eaten in three years. Which room is safest for him?

2. A man is wearing black. Black shoes, socks, trousers, coat, gloves, and ski mask. He is walking down a back street with all the streetlamps off. A black car is coming toward him, with its lights off, but somehow manages to stop in time. How did the driver see the man?

3. There are three lightbulbs inside a room, and outside are three light switches, each connected to one of the lights. Your job is to figure out which switch works which light, BUT you may only turn on two switches and you may only go inside the room once.

4. Before his death, a king leaves instructions that his son will take over his kingdom if he picks the correct note from inside a hat. The king arranges for his brother, the boy's uncle, to be in charge of this plan. On his father's death, the prince is told by his uncle that he must choose one of the two notes from the hat, and whichever note he chooses will determine his fate. On one note is written "Everything," on the other is written "Nothing." How does the prince win his kingdom?

5. On a bus, you can buy one ticket for $1 or a book of twelve tickets for $10. When a passenger gets on, she pays $10 and the bus driver immediately gives her a book of tickets. How did he know the passenger wanted a book of tickets and not a single ticket?

6. Can you draw a rectangle with three lines?

7. You're in a running race and you sprint forward and manage to overtake the second-
place runner. What position are you in now?

Try to answer the questions first. After you're
done, turn to page 221 for the answers. They seem
obvious once you're told, right? Sometimes we just
have to look at life from the other side, or even from
two sides.

Now let's test your creative thinking some more.

Take a look at this cylinder. Which side is the opening on?
Most people see it, at first, as going from left to right but, with
a bit of brain work, you can flip the image and look through the
opening on the right. It can take a little time to work out as you
instruct your brain to process the information in one way, and
then another way, instead of letting your brain choose for you.
Keep working that brain.

And now, what would you do in this situation? You have
a flight to take to an important business meeting. Your rental

car gets a flat tire. Not a problem, as your friend will drive you to the airport. But you need the car as soon as you return from your meeting that evening. You don't have much time so you think quickly and creatively, figuring out what Clunkers, the rental car agency, will need from you to get the problem fixed while you are away. Then, with all your plans prepared, you leave one friend with the car on the side of the road, hop into your other friend's car, set off for the airport and call Clunkers on your cell phone.

You explain your situation and are pleased to hear that the Clunkers service representative is helpful and responsive. "We'll be happy to send someone to change the tire or exchange the car." Good news. "And how long will that take?" you ask.

"Two hours. I'll need you to wait by your car for us, sir."

"Well, I can't do that as I'm on the way to the airport but I've left a friend by the car with the keys and all the documentation. He'll stay until the problem is fixed." You're feeling happy because you had the foresight to think about all this before leaving.

"I'm sorry, sir, but you have to wait by the car. Not your friend."

"But I can't do that as I'm in a car being driven to the airport. My other friend is waiting for you with everything you need."

"I understand, sir, but we need the officially registered person from the rental policy to be with the car."

"Should I cancel my flight, miss my meeting that might land me a TV show, and wait by the car?"

"I'm sorry, sir, I can't answer that question." Is this sounding familiar? You've probably been in a similar situation yourself. So what's to be done?

Maybe humor will fix the problem. "Let's say that I am waiting by the car for you. Is that okay? It is. What if another car comes along and hits me and I end up in the hospital with two broken legs? Then what? I can't be waiting for you by the car anymore. Would you change my tire then?"

"I'm sorry, sir, I can't answer that question." The right-side of my brain has been turned off for this exercise in customer service. I have been expressly forbidden from thinking outside the box.

So you've probably guessed that this scenario happened to me. My manager, Gary, sat in the car waiting for Clunkers while my other manager, Mike, drove me to the airport and I had my crazy phone call. Luckily, I eventually spoke to a supervisor who was able to answer my questions, get creative, and, with a conference call between her, me, and Gary, find a solution. Thinking creatively wins every time.

What if you heard a meteorologist say it was zero degrees Fahrenheit today and that tomorrow will be twice as cold? How would you work that out? How can you have twice as cold as zero degrees?

ANSWER:

Zero degrees Fahrenheit is the same as −17.77 degrees Celsius. Twice as cold would be −35.54 degrees Celsius, which would be −31.972 degrees Fahrenheit. This question is not really about getting the answer right. It's about the importance of thinking past the impossibility of the question. Being creative can be about thinking around a problem, not always looking at it head-on.

What about this one? If chocolate and chewing gum cost $1.10 together and the chocolate costs $1.00 more than the gum, how much does the gum cost?

You probably remember this one from the beginning of the book. Most people, when asked this question, answer, "10 cents." They get thrown off by the $1.00. But the key here is to realize that the chocolate costs $1.00 MORE, so if you say the gum costs 10 cents then the chocolate would have to cost $1.10 (and the chocolate and gum together would cost $1.20). The only possible answer is that the gum costs 5 cents, the chocolate $1.05, and together they cost $1.10. But you probably knew that now, because you've engaged your brain and become an expert.

One of my acts, as you know, is to ask someone to draw a picture on a sheet of paper while I am out of the room, drawing the shape by reading it in their mind. I've told you that most people draw the same thing. A smiley face. Are we really that lacking in creativity that we all draw the first thing that comes into our mind? How crazy is that? Crazy enough that I have to say, "Draw something, but please, do NOT draw a smiley face. I'd like to use my mental skills here!"

Now this may be hard for you to believe—especially if you're still thinking in a rational, left-brained kind of way—but the silliest, most ridiculous, nonsensical jokes can get you thinking creatively. Some of my favorite jokes are elephant jokes. They were a huge part of my childhood, and my friends and I can still sit around and cry with laughter over them. I love them for their surprise answers. And for their out-of-the-box logic. If you remember elephant jokes, then welcome back. If you've never heard them before, then you're in for a treat—while tuning your brain. I could tell you a hundred. Or more! But I'll keep it to a few less than that. The trick here is to keep your mind very wide-open to possibility, stay away from pure logic, and try to answer as quickly as possible. Have fun!

Q: How do you get four elephants into a Mini Cooper?
A: Two in the front and two in the back.

Q: How do you put an elephant in the fridge?
A: Open the fridge door, put the elephant in, and close the door.

Q: How do you put a giraffe in the fridge?
A: Open the fridge door, take out the elephant, put in the giraffe, and close the door.

Q: When the lion, King of the Animals, holds an important meeting in the jungle, which animal doesn't show up?
A: The giraffe. It's in the fridge.

Q: You're trying to cross the crocodile-filled river. How do you do it?
A: Swim. All the crocodiles are at the meeting.

Q: How do you know when there is an elephant in the fridge?
A: You hear it eating.

Q: How do you know when there are two elephants in the fridge?
A: You hear them talking.

Q: How do you know when there are four elephants in the fridge?
A: The Mini Cooper's parked outside.

Q: Why do elephants paint their toenails red?
A: To hide in fields of strawberries.

Q: Have you ever seen an elephant in a field of strawberries?
A: That means it's working . . .

Q: How do you prevent an elephant from slipping through the eye of a needle?
A: Tie a knot in his tail.

And the silliest one of all:

Q: Why are an elephant and a banana alike?
A: Because they're both yellow. Except the elephant.

You get the picture. Did you find yourself thinking of different answers? Or even coming up with the "right" answers? Good for you. You must be engaging both sides of your brain.

The Whole Brain at Work

I'm guessing you own a smart phone, or an iPod, or some other cool technological gadget, or at least know someone who does. You'll be amazed by how today's technology taps into the way we use our brains. Just over ten years ago, Apple introduced the first iPod. It was a revolutionary item in many ways—suddenly we could walk around with digitalized music in the palm of our hands—but a huge part of its appeal was its design and its marketing. It was cool and hip, on the cutting edge. Part of a lifestyle we all aspired to. And since that first iPod, Apple has introduced new generation after generation of iPods, and we've become more demanding as consumers—expecting the technological brilliance but also the beauty of the design. We expect fun and dazzling colors for our technology. We demand slimmer, lighter models. We're looking for aesthetic appeal. We no longer want computers or phones or music players that just process information and store photos—we want them to look good while doing so. Companies like Apple have put us in touch with the right side of our brains without us even knowing it. How often have you heard a computer geek gushing about their new iPad? It looks so beautiful. I had to buy it. I love the color. And then they'll rationalize about computer memory and megabytes and all those other reasons for buying it, when we all know that they bought it for emotional, aesthetic reasons.

Daniel Pink wrote an amazing book, *A Whole New Mind,*

which looks at whole-brain thinking in the U.S. workplace. His theory is that the days of left-brain dominance are over—those jobs that relied solely on rational, logical, sequential, computer-like thought processing are not the jobs of the future. Basic computer-coding, accounting, legal research, and financial analysis can all be done more cheaply overseas. Workers need to have a different mind-set for the future, a different way of thinking that includes innovation, inventiveness, and empathy as well. Right-brain qualities as well as left-brain.

So, the wave of the future seems to be employees tapping both sides of their brain in companies that encourage whole-brain thinking, in order to develop products and concepts for whole-brain-using consumers.

There's a cool story about a guy who became a millionaire. He put an advert in a newspaper, promising to send a tip on how to become a millionaire to anyone who sent him $1. He received $3 million from prospective millionaires and, as promised, he sent out a tip to all who had contacted him. The tip? A note saying, "Just do what I did!" And it was true, because even after paying for postage and supplies, he had still made over $1 million.

Speaking of creative millionaires, Google founders Larry Page and Sergey Brin built their company upon the vision that work should be challenging, and the challenge should be fun. The Google offices worldwide have gyms, yoga classes, pool tables, and video games. Brainstorming and idea-exchange happens in shared cubicles and huddle rooms—no solo offices. Every Friday, Larry and Sergey sit down at an all-company meeting, trading ideas, answering questions, and listening.

They introduced "20-percent time," to allow their engineers to spend a fifth of their workweek on projects that interest them but don't necessarily fall into their usual area of focus. Think of some of Google's best-known applications, like Gmail, Picasa, Google Maps, and Google Suggest; they all came out of this program. I'm guessing the people at Google aren't encouraged to say, "I'm sorry, I can't answer that question, sir."

As you know, the brand name "Google" has become a verb. We don't look things up in search engines on the Internet anymore, we Google them. In fact, the word "google" was officially *verbed* in the Oxford English Dictionary on June 15, 2006. And, by the way, Google is not pleased with this possible diluting of its brand. To me, it seems like a great marketing tool—like Uri Geller and his skeptics. For a little brain-flexing after all that reading, can you think of other brand names that have entered the mainstream as words? I'll start you off with Xerox. Can you think of others? How many? Ten? Twenty? Now let's see if you can get really creative and think of current brands that will become verbs in the next five years. What about brand Lior Suchard? As in, "Wow, you just pulled a Lior Suchard" instead of saying, "Wow, you just read my mind."

There's a story about creative thinking, which has always inspired me. At the age of fifty-two, Ray Kroc invested his life savings to become the exclusive distributor for the Multi-mixer, a milk-shake machine. When one of his clients, two brothers, ordered eight machines from him, his brain kicked into action and questioned, Why? Most clients only ordered one or two. Eight was unheard of. So Ray drove to San Bernardino, California, to investigate and found his clients running the busiest restaurant he had ever seen in his life. Its formula was quick, simple food: hamburgers, milk shakes, and fries. Ray was impressed—and his creative mind kicked into action again. He knew that this formula could be successful anywhere, and he suggested to the owners that they open up other restaurants—with his financial backing. The owners agreed, and the new restaurants were equally successful. By the way, the two brothers were called McDonald—and you know how the rest of the story goes. Creative thinking strikes again.

Gold Medal Thinking

Facebook founder Mark Zuckerberg works at an open desk in a big room full of engineers—no corner office for him. Whenever someone finishes up a big coding project, Zuckerberg bangs a gong in celebration.

Procter & Gamble just transformed their traditional R&D process by making it the company's goal to have 50 percent of its new products come from outside their own labs. They created a new job classification: technology entrepreneurs, who scout the world looking for scientific breakthroughs in university labs and research centers.

Nokia Corporation has introduced "Club 10," and inducts into it engineers with at least ten patents.

The company 3M grants "Genesis Grants" to scientists who would like to work on outside projects, awarding twelve to twenty grants each year, ranging from $50,000 to $100,000 each. Scientists use the money to take on extra staff and buy equipment for their new projects.

For my whole career, I've had to be creative. Being a mentalist is not the kind of job where you get up in the morning, go to work, and clock out at five P.M. No, mine is a job where I'm constantly thinking and asking questions: What comes next? What can I make happen next? Where is this going? How can I reinvent myself? Where can I go with this? Any time you have to ask yourself a lot of questions, you are forced to be creative. This is not a career where I have to think outside the box. It's a career where I throw away the box altogether. I find I'm constantly on the move, adapting myself to whatever life throws at me—and what I make life throw at me. Always reinventing myself: from entertainer at shows and private parties to infotainer. From entertainer on TV shows and talk shows to live entertainer in Las Vegas. From corporate ice-breaker to corporate detective. The world is always changing. I have to stay on my toes.

I'm always thinking of new ideas for my show, of new ways to showcase my mental skills. And some of them will fail. I know that. It makes sense that the more ideas you have, the more will fail. But failure isn't always bad. As Thomas Edison said, "I have not failed, I've just found ten thousand ways that won't work." One aspect of being creative is generating many,

many ideas, many possibilities. They won't all be great ideas, they might not even be good ideas, and some of them will not work as planned. But an idea that doesn't work can make you think in a different way, and sometimes that is what leads to the greatest successes. Creativity is a constant process. I think the best ideas and inventions come from a dream. I would like to do this, but how? How do I get to there? What are the steps? The possibilities? Then you take it from there—with every part of your mind at work.

This creative culture was in the air when I was growing up—it was exciting. My dad was always inventing, scribbling down ideas, working with his hands—like Leonardo da Vinci! My parents were perfectly fine letting me be the weird kid, the boy with the abilities. They didn't try to make me conform. They didn't force me to go to college. They knew that I had plans that definitely lay outside the box and they let me run with them. And I'm still running.

I think I'm lucky that I'm from Israel, where creativity has come to be really appreciated—especially in the last ten years. It's like it's a national gene. So many people there are entrepreneurs. Israel is a really small country, with about 7.5 million people. It has the largest number of high-tech start-up companies in absolute terms after the United States, and 80 percent of the three thousand Israeli companies involved in R&D are less than ten years old. There, being an entrepreneur has become a completely acceptable career choice—like being a doctor or a lawyer. It's easy for newcomers to get advice, as there are so many people involved that someone always knows a friend who has their own company. I, too, think of myself as an entrepreneur, a start-up—just me and the power of my mind.

It's interesting that a lot of the world's big companies—like Google, Intel, Microsoft—were all quick to open R&D centers in Israel—even during wars. The engineers and scientists there are expected to dream and think like crazy. I imagine them all full of people like me, jumping around with their minds on overload, saying, "Let's do this, let's do this, let's do this." And maybe one of the ideas will make it through and become the next worldwide hit. Like the cell phone, which was invented by Motorola R&D in Israel, or Intel computer chips, USB flash drives, or the world's tiniest camera for use in medicine. All invented in Israel. Google Suggest came from the Israeli team. You probably use it every day in Google without noticing; it's the list of suggestions that pops down when you type a request into the search box on the Google home page. I love it because it's a little bit like mind-reading. Google took the idea and developed it and now it's a household tool. Creative thinking at work.

I've been working on a brand-new act recently. One I'm really proud of. You've experienced some of it already, but now I'll tell you how it came into being, to really show my creative process at work. I like to keep things fresh, so that my show doesn't get stale or boring, for me as well as my audience.

Just like any artist, I live a normal life when I'm not performing. I have friends. I have a girlfriend. We go out to dinner and to the movies, and anything can be an inspiration for me for a new segment of my show. Even the color of a napkin could inspire me. But first, I have to set my rational thinking in place so that creativity can swoop in out of the blue. I'd been wanting to do something with phone numbers in my show for a long time; they're universal and yet personal. I've guessed people's phone numbers and PIN numbers in the past, but I wanted to include phone numbers in a longer segment that would weave throughout the performance and include several members of the audience.

So what could I do with a phone number that I hadn't done before? Whenever I'm thinking of new ideas, I try to come up with an impossible paradox. I dream big and then see what's possible. I wonder what will happen if I can get someone to choose a phone number out of an entire phone book—and I have predicted the number beforehand. So far so good. But not enough. Now what if we call that number and it connects to an answering machine that says, "Hi, thank you for calling. I hope you're enjoying Lior Suchard's show." That would be cool. But then I think, could I even do that? Is that possible? So I change tracks at this point. I still want to do something with numbers, and I like the idea of a random person choosing a random number from a phone book. So then I just let my mind wander off on its own and think. Every now and then, I'll come back to the problem and see if anything has resolved itself. What about social security numbers? Or dates of birth? No. My mind keeps on thinking while I go about other tasks.

So then, a couple of months after the idea started to form, I'm sitting in Vegas in a restaurant, paying my check. And then.

Boom. Out of the blue. An epiphany. There's the answer. Serial numbers on bills. I can combine phone numbers with serial numbers on money. So, all of a sudden, I have this idea where someone chooses a phone number, and someone else takes a dollar bill from their pocket, and the phone number and serial number on the bill match. How crazy is that? I love it. But I don't stop there. I want to go even further. I say to myself what else can we do with this? I want to improve, to create something amazing that will never be forgotten, something with triple coincidences, four climaxes, an impossible dream. And with creative thinking, I can do this.

Once I have the dream, I need to break it down, rationalize it, and say how can I make it happen? What are the steps and stages? Is this persuasion? Do I need to find other ways to do this? So I carefully plan it all out, and I practice parts of it, ironing out problems, smoothing out details until it works every time I try it. Only then can I add it to my show. But before I do that, I imagine myself sitting in the audience watching this part of my show. How does it look to an audience member? Where is the best place for me to stand? What are the best words to use? What about timing?

I think of myself as a director of the mind, controlling the whole thing. I think as the performer. I think as the spectator. I see each part of my act from the inside out. Does it show the amazing capabilities of the mind? Is it good entertainment? Will it engage the skeptics? Am I still growing as a mentalist? If so, then I'm happy with it. I'll take the new segment on the road with me.

An entire act will grow from one small thought from somewhere within the crazy reaches of my mind. But it doesn't grow on its own. I have to nurture it using every bit of brain power I have, and then—I unleash it on the world. Evidence of the amazing power of the mind.

Las Vegas, 2011

900 People

So we're back at my show. I've done all kinds of incredible things, guessed names, transferred energy, predicted a serial number on a bill that matched a randomly chosen phone number, and lots of other fantastic acts that you'll see when you come to one of my shows. There's been influencing and laughter, enjoyment and wonder. And now, just when the audience thinks that nothing else could possibly happen, there is more to come.

The show is almost over. It's been an amazing night. The positive energy is huge, sweeping across the audience, catching me up in it. The applause goes on and on, moving from one side of the room to the next, circling around. People are standing, their faces lit up with pleasure. I have my hand in the air, waiting for a slight pause. "There's just one more thing before you go," I shout. "Does anyone have a cell phone on them?" The audience is quiet now. They're thinking, could there possibly be something more? A man in the front row hands over his iPhone. "Thanks," I say and pretend to pocket it. Everyone laughs. I hand it back to him, saying so everyone can hear, "There's a phone number that was chosen tonight." I point at the flip chart. "Why don't we call it?"

"Sir," I say to the man with the iPhone. "Could you please call the phone number? On speakerphone, next to my microphone."

He dials the number and we hear the phone ring three times before it reaches an answering machine. A male voice comes on the line: "Thank you all for coming to see Supernatural Entertainment by Lior Suchard tonight. And a big thank-you to Blake and to Jane for their special help with the act."

Everyone is on their feet, almost in one move, the whole

audience, clapping and shouting, a sea of amazed faces, laughing, talking, exclaiming, and bubbling over with wonder. I hear individual voices here and there. One person shouts, "NO! That's impossible!" Someone else is just saying, "Oh my god, oh my god," over and over. Everyone shakes their heads in disbelief. I can hear people exclaiming, "That's crazy. How did he do that?" I know they'll be talking about it, wondering about it, long into the night and the days that follow. I can see it from the looks on their faces, the positive energy radiating from them. And I'm happy about that.

It's the power of persuasion. It's what I do.

So now you've experienced some of what I do. And now that you've read my book, guess what? The mind-reader is not just me. It's you, too.

Always think happy thoughts,
because you can never know
who's reading them.

Oh . . . I almost forgot. You remember the symbol you picked earlier on? It was impossible for me to know the numbers you'd choose and your final number, right? Well, I think I have a surprise for you. I told you I was going to read your mind. So I did. I think I know which symbol you chose. Turn the page. Am I right?

This symbol that you chose represents potential energy. We all have this inside us—we just have to believe in it to release it.

Now I also know that you will try it again . . . and you will have a surprise. So maybe it's not mind reading, but you can have fun with it and wow your friends and family. Let me know how it goes!

When I first saw this optical illusion, I was shocked. It's one of the best I've ever seen. Called the Jastrow illusion, it was discovered by the American psychologist Joseph Jastrow in 1889.

Think positively

Believe in yourself

Which shape do you think is bigger? Which do you think is more important? To think positively or to believe in yourself?

1. Take some scissors and cut around the two shapes exactly on the dotted line.
2. Place the shapes on the table, one below the other. Which is bigger? Which is more important? Believing in yourself, or thinking positively?
3. Now switch the places of the shapes. Which one is bigger now? Which one is more important?
4. Next put one shape on top of the other to compare.
5. NOW THEY ARE EQUAL—positive thinking and believing in yourself are equally important. Amazing, isn't it?

ANSWERS TO PROBLEMS ON PAGES 193–195

1. The third. Lions that haven't eaten in three years are dead.

2. It was daytime.

3. You turn on one switch and wait a couple of minutes, then you turn on another switch. Now you go inside the room. There will be two lit bulbs—one warm and one not. The unlit bulb corresponds to the unpressed switch. The warm bulb corresponds to the switch you pressed first, and the other lit bulb corresponds to the switch you pressed second.

4. The prince—like the king—knows that the uncle is a treacherous schemer who will try to make the prince

lose. So, the prince presumes that the uncle will put "Nothing" on both notes. He takes a note from the hat and swallows it. Then he looks at the remaining note, sees it says "Nothing," and claims the note he ate must have said "Everything." Therefore he wins his crown.

5. The passenger paid with ten $1 bills.

6. ┌─────────┐
   │ I I I │
   └─────────┘

7. Second. (Most people say first.)

ACKNOWLEDGMENTS

Many heartfelt thanks to my good friend Roi Yozevitch for spending long nights with me, helping me with ideas, thoughts, and stories. You're a superhero.

To my wonderful, one and only, Lindsey Tate. Thanks for your British sense of humor and kind heart, for laughing at elephant jokes at two o'clock in the morning and remaining calm when I began sentences twenty-four hours before our deadline with "I have another great idea for the book." I'm glad to have a writer and friend like you.

Thank you to Adam Korn for adopting the book with great enthusiasm, to Trish Daly for being able to see both the big picture and the tiny details, to Stephanie Meyers for a careful first edit, to Mauro DiPreta for taking a chance, to Frank Weimann for thinking there was a book in me, and, last but not least, to Gary and Mike for not stopping me when I shoot for the moon—I love you guys.

ABOUT THE AUTHOR

LIOR SUCHARD is a world-renowned entertainer and mentalist who first created a storm when he was selected as the winner of highly rated international TV show *The Successor,* hosted by celebrated mystifier Uri Geller. While amazing audiences with the power of his mind, Suchard appears often on international talk shows including *The Tonight Show with Jay Leno*, and he is a charismatic crowd-pleaser on the Las Vegas circuit.